Best Trail Runs
Portland, Oregon

BEST

TRAIL RUNS

PORTLAND, OREGON

ADAM CHASE | NANCY HOBBS | YASSINE DIBOUN

GUILFORD, CONNECTICUT

FALCONGUIDES®

An imprint of Globe Pequot
Falcon and FalconGuides are registered trademarks and Make Adventure Your
Story is a trademark of Rowman & Littlefield.

Distributed by NATIONAL BOOK NETWORK
Copyright © 2017 Rowman & Littlefield

Photos by Adam Chase and Nancy Hobbs unless otherwise noted
Maps: Melissa Baker © 2017 Rowman & Littlefield

British Library Cataloguing in Publication Information available

Library of Congress Cataloging-in-Publication Data available

ISBN 978-1-4930-2520-6 (paperback)
ISBN 978-1-4930-2521-3 (e-book)

♾™ The paper used in this publication meets the minimum requirements of
American National Standard for Information Sciences—Permanence of Paper for
Printed Library Materials, ANSI/NISO Z39.48-1992.

Printed in the United States of America

Contents

Beyond Portland

INTRODUCTION

INTRODUCTION
INTRODUCTION

FOREST PARK. That's about all you need to know to understand that Portland is a crown jewel in the royalty of trail-running capitals. Add the lush, verdant landscapes that make runners feel as though they are elves or hobbits running in a magical wonderland, on trails soft enough that your feet bounce rather than thud, and it is easy to get why Portland is a top-ranked destination for those wanting to run off-road.

It also explains why there are already several well-written, thoroughly researched trail-running guides for the area, and even more hiking guides for the same territory. And, really, what is the difference between a running trail and a hiking trail? With that many resources already available to trail runners seeking enticing trails to explore, what distinguishes this guide?

We didn't undertake this project because we thought we could do a "better" job than those who have written others but, rather, because we thought we'd bring new trails to light and that the presentation of trails we've selected for this book is written from a different and up-to-date perspective. In fact, that is what prompted us to recruit our friend, Yassine Diboun, a local who, as an accomplished ultrarunner, is extremely familiar with most every inch of Portland's trail system, to join us in putting together this guide. You've likely seen Yassine out on the trails, grin planted firmly on his face, as he trains and coaches other runners. Together with Yassine, it is our aim to provide you with fresh, new trails to accompany the traditional, sure-bet, can't-miss runs for the Portland area.

From Portland's city center you can travel in any direction and you are likely to find a trailhead before too long. Locals know the city by the "five quadrants": Northwest, Southwest, Northeast, Southeast, and North Portland. We know it doesn't make sense to have five sections as part of a quadrant, but this is one of the many "Keep Portland Weird" examples you'll discover in this unique city, dubbed "Portlandia." The Willamette

URBAN (PAVED) TRAILS IN PORTLAND

Because this is a "trail" running book, we have chosen to focus on true trails. The dirty kind. Accordingly, there is little discussion of paved paths, urban running segments, or "city trails," other than the select handful we've woven into the mix. There are, however, a few noteworthy urban corridors that are well-known, high-traffic trails in Portland:

- Springwater Corridor: This is an abandoned trolley route that was converted to a 21-mile paved path connecting downtown Portland with suburbs to the east. The Springwater Corridor runs next to Powell Butte, a location for trails featured in the book. We recommend asking about the safety of this area before you venture there for a run. For more information visit www.portlandoregon.gov/parks/finder/index.cfm?action=ViewPark&PropertyID=679.

- Southwest (SW) Trails: The Southwest Trails are a network of urban trail and road routes through Portland's Southwest hills. For more information visit https://swtrails.org; a map is at www.portlandoregon.gov/transportation/article/323776.

- The 40-Mile Loop: This network of trails, paved bike paths, and low-traffic roads connects to create a 40-mile loop around the Portland metro area. For more information visit http://40mileloop.org/wordpress/; a map is at http://40mileloop.org/wordpress/wp-content/uploads/2013/07/40mi-Loop_FINAL-for-Print_Page_1.jpg.

River divides the city from east and west, and Burnside Street separates north and south. North Portland is where the Willamette turns west and runs into the Columbia River (this river divides Oregon and Washington) and it creates a pie-shaped area. Vancouver Boulevard divides North and Northeast Portland. In this guide we have included areas and trailheads that extend into Washington, such as the Silver Star Mountain area, the Columbia River Gorge (Washington and Oregon), the Tillamook Forest (Oregon), and more.

It has been our objective, either through *The Ultimate Guide to Trail Running* or our roles with the American Trail Running Association, to help hikers accelerate to become trail runners, assist road runners to convert and adapt to trails, and provide direction for current trail runners to become stronger, more agile, and efficient. While we've been able to tackle the "how" in past work, this book allows us to take on the "where."

People who don't like precipitation shouldn't live in Stumptown, especially if they want to sport year-round tans. Chicken or egg is a good question, but Portland is US headquarters or home to some top-notch running and gear brands, adding emphasis to the saying that there's no such thing as bad weather, just bad gear or a bad attitude. Knowing your route and not being lost are great attitude enhancers and so, while we can't help you with the weather, we can help with that.

We can also provide some guidance on gear, training, nutrition, and preparedness. *Best Trail Runs Portland* addresses running on wet ground and through water and mud, and the related concerns of exposure, traction, and other safety factors. The guide also discusses gear choices for addressing the various weather conditions you are likely to face on the trails we've included. Given our positions with the American Trail Running Association, we've also incorporated a discussion of when not to run on muddy trails, and environmental concerns that are unique to Portland trail running.

DIFFICULTY RATINGS

Being that many trail runners are also Alpine skiers who understand the meaning of easy/green, intermediate (moderate)/blue, and difficult/black for rating the difficulty of a run, we chose to go with that for the trails in this book. We acknowledge the subjective nature of this, noting that one person's hard is another's easy, but we did want to guide readers with some sense of relative ease or difficulty so that they may plan accordingly.

CELL PHONE COVERAGE

We also deemed it helpful to readers to know if a trail has cell phone coverage. This is merely for safety purposes. We urge trail runners to use proper etiquette and to refrain from using phones, except in cases of emergency or to take pictures of the beautiful scenery through which these trails run.

Getting Started

Whereas road running is a more straightforward, linear function, trail training is multidimensional because it blends lateral motion with forward movement. To adapt your training routine to accommodate varying terrain inherent in trails, you will need to focus on strengthening your stabilizing muscles and balance. Similarly, because you will surely encounter hills—both steep climbs and steady climbs—as a trail runner, you should consider the benefits of including training workouts that focus on strength, such as running hill repeats of varying intervals and distance. If you want to become a faster and fitter trail runner, you should consider increasing your speed through repeats, improving your fitness by running intervals and speed drills, and, finally, you may want to hit the weight room and incorporate a stretching regime.

It is not very easy to find a flat trail in Portland. True, the flat trail does exist, but given its relative rarity, trail runners in the Portland metropolitan area become quickly and painfully aware of the importance and benefits of hill training.

Pacing or economy of effort are probably the most important aspects of effective hill running. Much to their regret, novice trail runners are frequently less inclined (no pun intended) to use appropriate pacing on hills. As a result, they face the consequences of sputtering out with burning calves, huffing lungs, and possibly even nausea long before reaching the summit. Those new to hilly trails also tend to use improper form when descending and, accordingly, suffer from aching quadriceps and knee joints.

Running hills efficiently is a skill acquired through a process of fine-tuning and lots of practice, accounting for differences in body type, strength, weaknesses, agility, fitness, and aversion to risk. Armed with proper technique, a trail runner is prepared to take on hills—or mountains, for that matter—with alacrity instead of dread.

Whether you should attack with speed or power hike a hill or steep ascent is a complex decision that depends on the length of the climb, the trail surface, your level of fatigue, the altitude, the distance of the run, at what point in the run you encounter the hill, and whether you are training or racing. Efficient power hiking is often faster than running, especially in longer runs, when the footing is difficult, or at high altitude. It can be very rewarding to hike past someone who is trying to run up a hill, and know that you are expending far less effort while you move at a faster pace. Conversely, it is quite demoralizing to be passed by a hiker while you struggle to run up a steep incline.

Two crucial elements of being a strong hill runner are tempo and confidence. A runner who is able to maintain tempo, cadence, or rhythm ascending and descending a hill will be more efficient and generally faster on hills than a runner who tries to muscle up and down the same slope in fits and starts. Two secrets to maintaining your tempo on a hill are the discipline and ability to adjust stride length.

Observing the fastest and most efficient climbers, both human and animal, it is easy to note their sustained turnover with a shortened stride on the climb. Even speedy mountain types go slower uphill and faster downhill, but the cadence of their legs hardly changes, regardless of the grade, the only difference being stride length. Just as you shift into lower gear when you bicycle up a hill, you need to shift gears as a runner by shortening your stride length.

A short stride on both the ascent and descent works very well on trails that are particularly rugged with difficult footing. By using many little steps, you are able to make quick adjustments to correct your footing on the fly. That allows you the most sure-footed landing, for better traction and control. The ability to alter your path increases both your real and perceived control, which leads to a greater confidence, especially on descents. A heightened level of confidence on hills leads to a "heads-up" running style.

Proper form and confidence on hills increases a runner's enjoyment of inclines and declines and, at the same time, decreases the chances of injury. With more confidence, you will be able to relax and run with a lighter, more flowing form that is more efficient and less painful. Knowing how to confront hills will keep you coming back for more, and because training on hills, whether on long, sustained ascents or shorter hill repeats, presents a superb opportunity for running-specific strength training, you will become a stronger and more confident runner overall.

Trail Training

Compared with road running, trail running requires a more balanced and comprehensive approach, incorporating the whole body. Trail runners must be prepared to handle varying terrain, conditions, steep inclines and declines, and other challenges not found on the road. Fortunately, one thing trail runners don't need to train for is dealing with motorized vehicles.

Although many of the following training techniques apply to road running, it is also necessary to perform them on trails if your goal is to become a better, more accomplished trail runner. Yes, you may become a faster road runner by doing speed work on the track; but that speed does not always transfer to trails, where you will be forced to use a different stride, constantly adjust your tempo for frequent gear changes, and maintain control while altering your body position to stay upright.

DISTANCE TRAINING

If your goal is to run or race a certain distance, then training for that distance will be a mandatory building block in your trail training regimen.

Incorporating long runs into weekly training will help your body adjust physiologically to the increased impact-loading stress by generating more bone calcium deposits, and by building more and stronger leg muscles and connective tissue. Building up weekly mileage improves your aerobic capacity to generate a base upon which you can mix speed and strength training runs into your schedule.

Long training runs enable your body to cope with high mileage by breaking down fats for fuel and becoming more biomechanically efficient. Psychologically, long runs teach you to cope with and understand fatigue. During lengthy training runs, runners frequently experience what can become an emotional roller coaster. It is useful to become familiar with how you respond under such circumstances, especially if you are training for a longer distance trail race. Long runs also help build confidence as a measure of progress. And, perhaps best, these runs become adventures into unchartered territory, allowing you to explore new stretches of trails and see new sites.

Some simple advice for those converting from roads to trails—especially for those who keep a log to record time, distance, and pace—is to forget about training distance or, if you know the distance of a trail, leave your watch behind when you go for a training run. Since trail running is invariably slower than road running, you will only get frustrated if you make the common mistake of comparing your trail pace with your road or track pace.

A prime reason for running trails is to escape tedious calculations, so free yourself from distance and time constraints, and just run and enjoy, particularly during your initial exposure to trail running. Tap into the wonderful feeling of breezing by brush and trees as you flow up and down hills and maneuver sharp corners with skill and agility. You can always fret about your pace as you develop your trail skills and speed.

If you base your trail running training on the premise that long runs are primarily a function of time rather than ground covered, you should keep training runs close to the amount of time you think it will take to run your target distance. For example, if you are training to complete a 5.0-mile trail run in the near future, you might set your training run for 45 minutes. If, however, you are training for a trail marathon or ultramarathon, you probably want to keep your distance training to somewhat less than the time it will take you to complete the race distance. To get to that point, you may want to set aside between one day every two weeks to two days a week for long runs, depending on your goal, experience, fitness background, and resistance to injury.

Trail runners usually dedicate one day of the week for a considerably longer training run, although some prefer to run two relatively long days back-to-back, especially on weekends when their schedules are more accommodating. This latter training method, known as a "brick workout," is common among ultramarathoners who must condition their bodies to perform while tired and stressed. Newer runners should not try brick workouts until they are both comfortable with trails and are confident that their bodies will be able to withstand two days of long runs without breaking down or suffering an injury.

Because the forgiving surface of trails, especially those in the Portland area, may allow a person to run relatively injury-free, newer trail runners are often lulled into building up their distance base with long runs too rapidly. Whether performed on road or trail, distance running takes its toll on the body, and too quick an increase in distance often leads to injury, burnout, or leaving yourself prone to illness due to a compromised immune system. Depending on age, experience with endurance athletics in general, and your running history, it is better to increase your mileage or hours by no more than 5 to 10 percent per week.

Even if you increase your mileage base gradually, do not forfeit quality for quantity. Many runners succumb to the unhealthy game of comparing weekly mileages with either their previous weeks or with those of other runners. Junk miles are just that. Depending on your objectives, it is usually better to run fewer miles with fresher legs and at a more intense pace than to slog through miles merely to rack them up in your logbook.

One way to check the quality of your miles is to wear a heart rate monitor, and couple the distance of your runs with the goal of staying within your training zone at a steady pace. If you find your heart rate consistently rising above or falling below that target rate as you tack on the miles, that is a sign you are overtraining; and it is unlikely you will derive much benefit from those miles unless you are training for ultradistance.

SPEED TRAINING

For some trail runners, just being out on the trails and communing with nature is enough. They don't care about their pace. Others want to increase their speed. Building up your distance base should help increase your running speed; but it only helps to a certain extent. To really pick it up and break through the barrier of your training pace, you should run fast. Running at a faster pace helps improve both cardiovascular fitness and biomechanical efficiency.

This discussion, however, is aimed at those who find it more exhilarating to push their limits, who enjoy the feeling of rushing along a wooded path, and who appreciate the fitness improvements that result from challenging themselves.

Beyond velocity, speed training—whether through intervals, repeats, tempo runs, fartleks, or other means—has positive physiological effects. Pushing the pace forces muscles and energy systems to adapt to the more strenuous effort. The body does this by improving the flow of blood to muscles, increasing the number of capillaries in muscle fiber, stimulating your muscles to increase their myoglobin and mitochondria content, and raising aerobic enzyme activity to allow muscles to produce more energy aerobically.

Running fast also provides a mental edge, because psychologically—if you are familiar with the stress and burning sensation known to many as "pain and suffering" that accompany running at a faster-than-normal pace during training—you will be able to draw from that experience and dig deeper into your reserves when needed during a race. Speed training on trails also forces you to push your comfort level with respect to the risk of falling or otherwise losing control on difficult terrain. Pushing the envelope helps establish a sense of confidence that is crucial to running difficult sections, especially descents, at speed.

Breaking away from the daily training pace and pushing oneself shakes up the routine and rejuvenates muscular, energy, and cardiovascular systems so that one may reprogram for a faster pace with more rapid leg speed and foot turnover. Running at a quicker pace than normal helps to realign running form and teaches respect for different speeds.

However, because speed training is an advanced form of training, it should not be introduced into one's routine before establishing a consistent training base. Beginning trail runners should start by becoming comfortable with running on trails before they endeavor to run those trails fast. Speed training stresses the body so it may be wise to do your faster workouts on tamer trails with dependable footing, dirt roads, or even a track or road.

INTERVALS

Although interval training improves leg speed, its primary goal is cardiovascular—to optimize lactate threshold. As an anaerobic training tool, intervals are designed to increase a runner's ability to maintain a fast pace for a longer period of time. Without an improvement in lactate threshold, the runner will be unable to run or race a substantial distance at a faster pace than the rate at which the body can comfortably use oxygen, thereby causing lactate to form in the bloodstream. Intervals help to raise the level at which the body begins the lactate production process so that the runner is able to run faster and longer without feeling muscles burn or cramp. Upon developing a substantial training base of endurance, speed intervals allow acceleration of pace and an increase in overall running fitness.

Intervals are usually measured in terms of time rather than distance, especially if run on hilly or rugged trails. During the "on" or hard-effort segments of interval training, trail runners should work hard enough to go anaerobic (i.e., faster than your lactate or anaerobic threshold so that the body goes into oxygen debt). During the "off" or recovery segments, you are allowed to repay some of the oxygen debt, but not all of it. The rest period should be sufficiently short so that you are "on" again before full recovery.

An interval workout may be a series of equal on-and-off interval and recovery periods, or a mix of different length intervals and recoveries. For example, a trail runner might run six intervals of four minutes each, interspersed with three-minute recoveries. Alternatively, the interval session might mix it up with five-, four-, three-, two-, three-, four-, and five-minute intervals, each separated by a three-minute recovery.

Intervals may be as long as six minutes and as short as thirty seconds. Run intervals at a pace that is a bit faster than lactate threshold, which is usually equivalent to the pace run when racing a distance from 2 miles to 5 kilometers in length. The interval pace should be uncomfortable, but not excruciating; although not a sprint, you should feel you are running fast.

Run longer intervals if training for longer distances, and shorter intervals if speed is the goal. The off (recovery) period between intervals is an active rest that ranges between jogging and moderate running. Recovery time should be a little shorter than the time of the interval preceding it. In addition to recoveries between the intervals, any interval workout should integrate a substantial warm-up before and cooldown after running.

HILL REPEATS AND REPETITION WORKOUTS

"Repeats" resemble intervals, except that leg speed and strength are emphasized more than lactate threshold (although repetition workouts have some beneficial lactate threshold effects). Put another way, repeat workouts are designed for biomechanical and physiological improvement more than for cardiovascular benefits. Hill repeats are intended to hone your climbing skills, and generally make for a stronger runner by taxing the muscular system with anaerobic intervals.

Repeats are run at, or faster than, the lactate threshold pace, and each interval is shorter in length than in a standard interval workout. Typically, repeats last two minutes or less; and because repeats are more intense than intervals, the recovery period is longer. Since the focus is muscle strength improvement rather than fitness, the active rest between repeats should be long enough to recharge and prepare for the next repeat at or above lactate threshold. In short, if you run a two-minute repeat and need three minutes to recover, take the full three minutes. You want to recover enough to make each repeat interval sufficiently intense to realize the full benefits of the exercise.

Run each interval at a pace that you can maintain through the entire repeat workout. Don't push so hard during early repeats that you are unable to finish the rest of the workout. Hill repeats provide a great strength and lactate threshold workout with minimal stress to the body, because you push hard to go anaerobic while climbing, but then rest as you slowly jog or walk to the bottom of the hill. Because of the reduced stress, you can throw hill repeats into your training schedule on a weekly basis without jeopardizing the health of your connective tissue.

TEMPO RUNS

Imagine a spectrum, with repeats that focus on biomechanics and muscular strength buildup at one end, intervals that focus on a combination of lactate threshold and biomechanics in the middle, and tempo runs at the other end, which emphasize lactate threshold or cardiovascular fitness.

Repeats	Intervals	Tempo Runs
Biomechanics/Strength		**Cardio/Lactate Threshold**

Tempo runs are sustained efforts at an even pace, usually lasting 20 to 40 minutes; although those training for longer distances may do tempo runs that stretch to 90 minutes. The pace should be a lactate threshold pace, which is faster than the pace at which you are able to maintain a conversation, but not faster than one that forces you to exceed 90 percent of maximum heart rate. The pace could be maintained for about an hour, if racing. Since the goal of tempo training is to maintain a steady pace with consistent leg turnover, run tempos on a trail or dirt road that is relatively flat with good footing.

Tempo runs should include a warm-up and cooldown, both at a comfortable pace. If the tempo workout involves training partners, be careful to not turn the session into a race or time trial. To prevent that from occurring, wear a heart rate monitor and set it to sound an alarm if the heart rate rises above lactate threshold rate. Because tempo runs are physiological workouts, the goal is to run at a certain effort rather than to cover a certain distance. Depending on terrain, weather, or how rested you are beginning a tempo run, the pace may vary, but the body should nevertheless be working at threshold level throughout the workout.

Because considerable concentration and focus are required to maintain a steady lactate threshold pace for 20 minutes or longer, runners frequently find themselves a bit tired, both physically and mentally, the next day or two after a tempo workout. If that is the case, take a day of active rest or work a recovery run into your schedule. It may even be advisable to take the next day off to rest up and maintain trail running vigor.

FARTLEKS

Fartlek is Swedish for "speed play." Scandinavians, known for their trail running prowess and long history in the sport, pioneered the art of running fast on trails. Fartleks are creative workouts that weave a variety of paces into the same run. Although fartleks can be performed solo, they are often run as a group, in single file with the leader setting the pace—sometimes sprinting, sometimes jogging, sometimes walking, at other times simply running. Because the pace of a fartlek often varies with the terrain, these invigorating workouts are most successful if run on trails that offer a mix of short and long hills, and plenty of turns and obstacles.

Fartleks offer a fun alternative to more standardized, timed speed workouts. Because they lack any regimented order, fartleks can reinject zip into a training routine that has grown boring, or introduce some excitement when running feels lethargic. The pacesetter can rotate, and faster runners may loop back to pick up stragglers to keep the fartlek group intact.

To capture some benefits of a fartlek when running alone, throw in some surges to get some speed training. Surges are short blasts of speed worked into a training run to accentuate a transition in the trail, such as near the top of a hill or at the bottom of a hill when beginning a climb.

Another way to mix training with a little speed is to integrate striders or accelerations into the routine. An excellent time to insert some striders or accelerations is at the end of a trail run, just before the cooldown. Striders and accelerations are usually performed on flat, soft surfaces such as grassy parks, playing fields, or dirt roads. If striders or accelerations are run on grass or sand, try removing shoes so as to work on the muscle tone of lower legs and feet while feeling light and free. Strider and acceleration distances should range between 50 and 100 meters, allowing for an additional 10 meters to get started and 20 to 30 meters to slow down.

A strider is usually run at a fast running pace, just under or even finishing with a sprint. Place emphasis on high knee lifts and getting a full kick off each step so as to cover as much ground as possible without overstriding. When striding, think of sprinters warming up on a track, swinging arms and lifting knees in an accentuated manner. Accelerations resemble striders, but begin more slowly and end in a full sprint.

"OFF-TRAIL" SPEED TRAINING

Although the goal of speed training is to improve physiology, the cardiovascular system, biomechanics, the muscular system, and mental strength, it is not necessary to do all speed training on trails. In fact, it is more effective to perform some speed training sessions on the track, dirt roads, or even paved roads. Depending on where you live and the types of trails to which you have access, it may be a lot easier to do speed training off the trails, reserving the trip to trails for longer runs.

Road and track are better suited for certain types of speed training. Tempo runs, where the focus is on a steady pace, and repeats, where the emphasis is on leg turnover, should be performed on flatter, more dependable surfaces. Roads or tracks are certainly easier than the trail for these types of workouts, especially if trails are icy or muddy.

Track sessions tend to be highly efficient. Perhaps it is the lane lines or the bends of the turns, but something about running on a track creates a feeling of running fast. That feeling may well convert to actual speed, which means a more effective speed session. Tracks are also a helpful option because they are measured for convenient pacing. If you want to do repeats or intervals and maintain a set pace, going to the track is an efficient alternative to the trail.

In addition to selecting the appropriate speed workout and venue for the session, also take the weather into consideration. If it is snowy, icy, muddy, or particularly windy, it may not be possible to get a good speed workout outside. Depending on training needs and personal preferences, train inside and run a set of repeats or intervals on the treadmill, or work on leg turnover with some spinning. However, many trail runners are adamantly opposed to such mechanical alternatives and insist on running outside, regardless of the weather. That is fine and well, but they then must be willing to either forego speed training sessions when the weather is particularly nasty, or attempt to do them in unfavorable conditions.

PORTLAND

NORTH PORTLAND

CATHEDRAL PARK TO FOREST PARK

THE RUN DOWN

START: Cathedral Park; elevation 33 feet

OVERALL DISTANCE: 6.7 miles out and back

APPROXIMATE RUNNING TIME: 90 minutes

DIFFICULTY: Blue

ELEVATION GAIN: 1,437 feet

BEST SEASON TO RUN: Year-round

DOG FRIENDLY: Leashed dogs permitted

PARKING: Free

OTHER USERS: Equestrians and bikes on designated trails

CELL PHONE COVERAGE: Good

MORE INFORMATION: www .forestparkconservancy.org/ forest-park/facts/

FINDING THE TRAILHEAD

There is parking at Cathedral Park, which is about three-quarters of a mile from the trailhead. From the junction at St. Johns Bridge and Forest Park, you will see a concrete staircase that goes up to the trailhead at Ridge Trail.

RUN DESCRIPTION

This "twofer" out-and-back run double-dips into Portland's precious parks. The run begins and ends at Cathedral Park, and includes Forest Park and the St. Johns Bridge, for a real mélange of Portland in relatively short order. This run is a favorite of the University of Portland cross-country team.

A well-deserved moniker, Cathedral Park gets its name from the religious feel you get looking up at the architecturally compelling arched

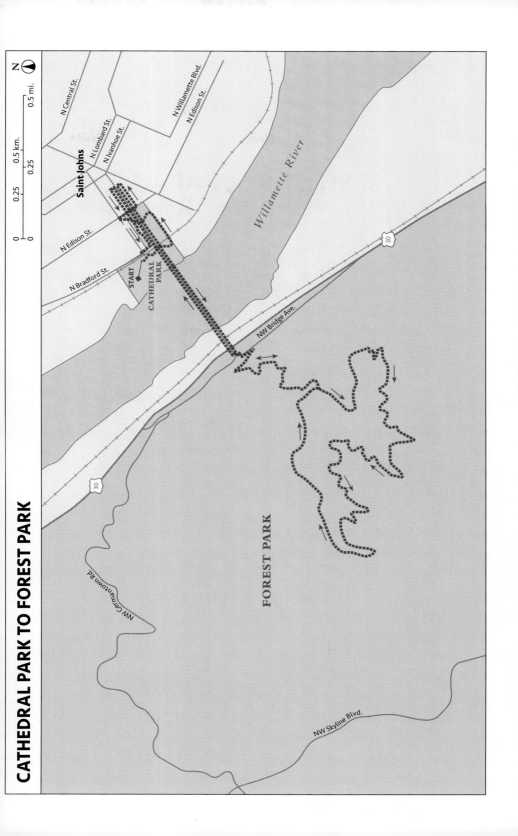

CATHEDRAL PARK TO FOREST PARK

underbelly of the historic St. Johns Bridge. It may also be a religious experience for those afraid of heights because it is not for the faint of heart, given its high rise over the Willamette River. You can start the run after a coffee at nearby Cathedral Coffee, 7530 N. Willamette Boulevard, and celebrate the outing by hitting Occidental Brewing Company, 6635 N. Baltimore Avenue #102, just across the street from the park.

This is a hybrid road, "urban trail," and more traditional trail run and makes a good starter run for someone new to trails but not necessarily new to running. It begins and ends on pavement, running on the asphalt path that leaves Cathedral Park. Head up and across the St. Johns Bridge to the entry of Forest Park off of Northwest Bridge Avenue, and then onto Ridge Trail, which you'll need to look for on your left and up from the intersection. From the entrance, make a winding ascent to Northwest Leif Erikson Drive, where you take a right on the road, following the pavement until it takes a hard right, where Hardesty Trail breaks off to the left.

Follow the Hardesty Trail for a short spell, and then take a left onto Wildwood Trail. Stay on Wildwood, passing across Ridge Trail and zig-zagging your way down to bear left at Gasline Trail briefly, before taking a left to connect to Leif Erikson Drive, which takes you back to Ridge Trail, where you started the loop.

After completing the loop, return the way you came, following Ridge Trail to Northwest Bridge Avenue, then running back onto the bridge and across to Cathedral Park.

PIER PARK/CHIMNEY PARK 5K

Pier Park and Chimney Park are adjacent parks in the City of Portland parks system. Pier Park is the larger of the two, with 87 acres, while Chimney Park has less than 20 acres. There are paved and unpaved pathways in the parks, passing in and out of pine forests and meadows, as well as opportunities for other activities including an off-leash dog park, disc golf, picnicking, and more. The area is also home to cross-country races in the fall. Pier Park is a filming location for the NBC network television series *Grimm*.

THE RUN DOWN

START: Pier Park TriMet stop; elevation 95 feet

OVERALL DISTANCE: 3.3-mile double loop, retracing some steps

APPROXIMATE RUNNING TIME: 40 minutes

DIFFICULTY: Green

ELEVATION GAIN: 400 feet

BEST SEASON TO RUN: Year-round

DOG FRIENDLY: Leashed dogs permitted

PARKING: A fee is charged

OTHER USERS: Bikers; no equestrians

CELL PHONE COVERAGE: Good

MORE INFORMATION: www
.portlandoregon.gov/parks/
finder/index.cfm?propertyid=
513&action=ViewPark

FINDING THE TRAILHEAD

If taking a bus, choose number 44 or 75, and disembark at the Pier Park TriMet stop. The stop is within Pier Park. By car, take North Lombard Street from the St. John's neighborhood west to the park. Street parking is adjacent to the park in the neighborhood.

RUN DESCRIPTION

Start this route at the Pier Park TriMet stop located near the baseball diamonds within the park. The route is partially on grass around the

PIER PARK/CHIMNEY PARK 5K

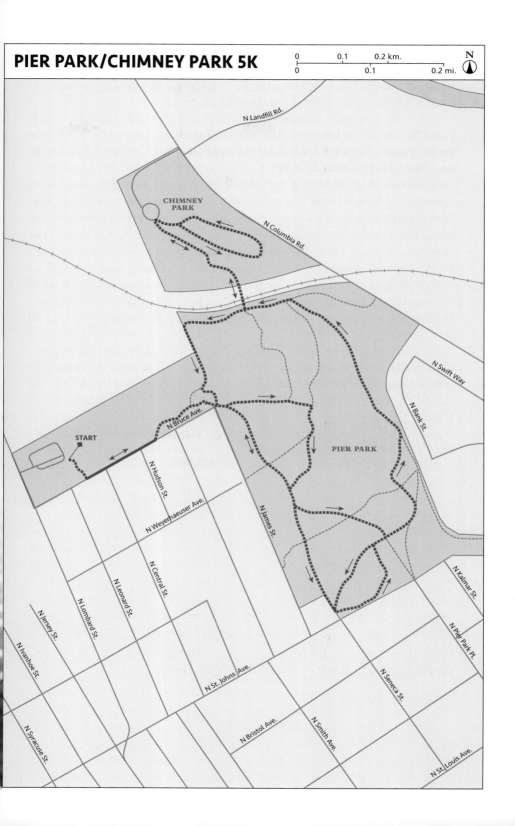

periphery of the ball fields, and utilizes singletrack and double-track, pine-needle-strewn trails throughout the park.

Pier Park is densely packed with formal and informal trails and quite contained, so if you happen to stray from this route, worry not: Ad lib and know you can't really get lost because the park is quite small, at only 87 acres with clearly defined borders.

From Pier Park, head to North Bruce Avenue and head left, past North Central and North Hudson Streets, before reentering the park on the Pier Park Trail to your left. Follow the trail around the inside corner of the park, past the juncture of North Bruce and North James, heading to the right on Pier Park Trail. There are three inner loops on the Pier Park Trail or, if you want a shorter run, just stay on the perimeter trail throughout and circumnavigate the park. As you are heading back toward the baseball diamonds, you can also add a short lollipop by crossing over a set of tracks to Chimney Park and running the dog park loop before heading back to your starting point.

For some java after the run, consider Two Stroke Coffee, at 8926 N. Lombard Street, or SOMA Kombucha Speakeasy, at 7319 N. John Avenue If it's lunch fare, stop in at Signal Station Pizza, 8302 N. Lombard Street.

STRENGTH TRAINING

The image of a road runner is often that of the ectomorph—somewhat bony with elongated muscles and perhaps a sunken chest. Without besmirching those who restrict their running to paved surfaces, it can be said that trail runners tend to be a bit more muscular and "shapely" than their roadie equivalents. Many reasons account for the differences, but an important one concerns the trail runner's proclivity to vary exercise and recreation routines with other sports, many of which build strength and use the runner's upper body.

When not running, trail runners tend to gravitate toward recreational activities such as backpacking, rock climbing, swimming or pool running, mountain biking, kayaking, backcountry skiing, rollerblading, or even horseback riding. These other disciplines build strength and draw on muscles that are less often, or not often, used when running. Many trail runners alter workouts to combine trail running and at least one other outdoor activity. For example, a trail runner might run to the base of a mountain to do some bouldering, or mountain bike to a remote trail system, then quickly transition to running.

Trail runners can complement and enhance running strength with resistance training. Given that trail running draws from a broad range of muscles, the balance derived from regularly hitting the weight room, as well as including a core strength program, can have considerable performance-enhancing benefits, on and off the trail. Not only can you gain strength for speed and hill climbing through resistance training, but it serves to prevent injury, increase resting metabolism, align and balance muscles for improved biomechanics, and build tendon and ligament strength.

NORTHEAST PORTLAND
I-205 PATHWAY TO ROCKY BUTTE TRAIL

THE RUN DOWN

START: Gateway MAX station; elevation 285 feet

OVERALL DISTANCE: 7.6 miles out and back (with loop)

APPROXIMATE RUNNING TIME: 80 minutes

DIFFICULTY: Blue

ELEVATION GAIN: 892 feet

BEST SEASON TO RUN: Year-round

DOG FRIENDLY: Leashed dogs permitted

PARKING: Free

OTHER USERS: Cyclists

CELL PHONE COVERAGE: Good

MORE INFORMATION: www.oregonhikers.org/field_guide/Rocky_Butte_Hike

FINDING THE TRAILHEAD

Park at either the Gateway MAX station at 1321 NE 99th Avenue or at the Fred Meyer shopping center. The I-205 Multi-Use Path is located just west of the Gateway MAX station and heads north and south. For this route, head north (right).

RUN DESCRIPTION

This route features gnarly singletrack, dirt road, paved bike path, and a few short road sections.

Starting at the end of NE Pacific Street, get on the I-205 corridor path and head to your right, along the Veterans Memorial Highway/I-205. Bear to your right on the Gateway Green Trail after crossing under the T. H. Banfield Freeway and NE Halsey Street, until the path eventually rejoins the

ROCKY BUTTE CITY PARK

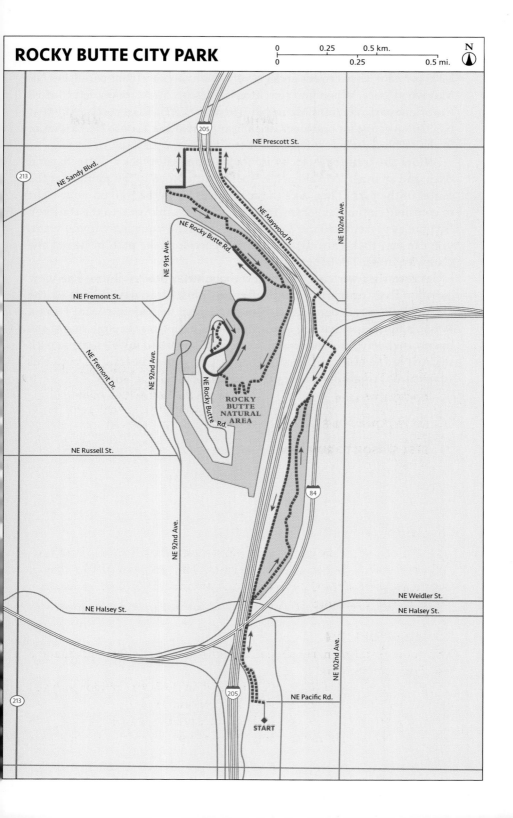

0   0.25   0.5 km.
0   0.25   0.5 mi.

N

NE 205

NE Prescott St.

NE 213

NE Sandy Blvd.

NE Maywood Pl.

NE Rocky Butte Rd.

NE 91st Ave.

NE 102nd Ave.

NE Fremont St.

NE Fremont Dr.

NE 92nd Ave.

NE Rocky Butte Rd.

ROCKY
BUTTE
NATURAL
AREA

NE Russell St.

NE 92nd Ave.

84

NE Weidler St.

NE Halsey St.

NE Halsey St.

NE 213

205

NE 102nd Ave.

NE Pacific Rd.

START

I-205 corridor, then crosses under several highways and runs parallel to NE Maywood Place. When you run into NE Prescott Street, take a left to cross the bridge over Veterans Memorial Highway/I-205. Take your next left at NE 92nd Avenue for one block, then bear right at the T, onto NE Skidmore for half a block, where you'll see the trailhead on your left.

Follow the trail for a clockwise loop around the Rocky Butte Natural Area, and an inner loop along NE Rocky Butte Road to the summit, at the center of the park. Then take the road back to join the trail on your right to continue circumnavigating the natural area. Link back to the trail you first ran as you entered the natural area, retracing your steps. If you want, you can run back entirely on the I-205 corridor bike path in lieu of the Gateway Green Trail, for variety.

Get rewarded with a view from the summit of Rocky Butte. The view corridor faces primarily north offering—on a clear day—views of the Columbia River, Mount Hood, Mount Rainier, and Mount Saint Helens. What is notable is that the I-205 Multi-Use Path runs through one of the busiest highway interchanges in Portland. The trail follows a narrow park situated in the heart of this interchange. Get your city-trail fix with this adventurous route along bike paths, sidewalks, and singletrack.

ROCKY BUTTE GROTTO TRAIL RUN

THE RUN DOWN

START: The Grotto; elevation 220 feet

OVERALL DISTANCE: 3.8 miles out and back

APPROXIMATE RUNNING TIME: 50 minutes

DIFFICULTY: Green

ELEVATION GAIN: 679 feet

BEST SEASON TO RUN: Year-round

DOG FRIENDLY: Dogs on leash on Rocky Butte, but no dogs permitted in the Grotto

PARKING: Free

OTHER USERS: Bikers; no equestrians

CELL PHONE COVERAGE: Good

MORE INFORMATION: www .oregonhikers.org/field_guide/ Rocky_Butte_Hike

FINDING THE TRAILHEAD

Start at the Grotto (8840 NE Skidmore Street), a cliff-side Catholic sanctuary known for its Pieta replica in a grotto and serene botanical gardens. From the Grotto, head east on NE Skidmore Street, and the trail is on the right.

RUN DESCRIPTION

Rocky Butte has a rich geological history. This route enables you to experience that history through many buildings and vantage points, as well as at the visitor center in the Grotto. This route is a shorter version of the I-205 Multi-Use/Rocky Butte run described above—sans the I-205 portion. This out-and-back route is on paved and unpaved pathways in and out of forested terrain. From the summit, on a clear day runners will be rewarded with views of Mount Saint Helens to the north, and the Columbia Gorge to the east, as well as Mount Hood.

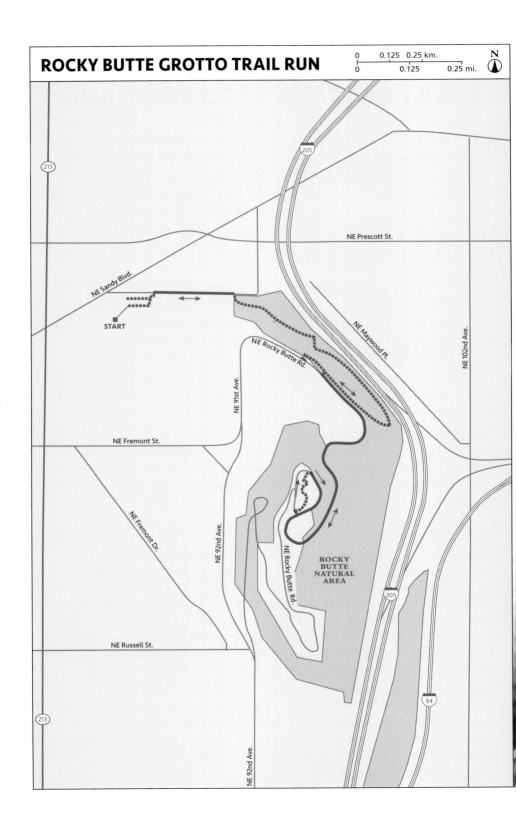

ROCKY BUTTE GROTTO TRAIL RUN

0   0.125   0.25 km.

0   0.125   0.25 mi.

N

213

NE Prescott St.

205

NE Sandy Blvd.

START

NE Rocky Butte Rd.

NE Maywood Pl.

NE 102nd Ave.

NE 91st Ave.

NE Fremont St.

NE 92nd Ave.

NE Fremont Dr.

NE Rocky Butte Rd.

ROCKY
BUTTE
NATURAL
AREA

205

NE Russell St.

84

213

NE 92nd Ave.

From the Grotto, run east, along NE Skidmore Street, until you reach the trailhead on your right. Run a clockwise loop around the Rocky Butte Natural Area and an inner loop along NE Rocky Butte Road to the summit, at the center of the park. Then take the road back to join the trail on your right to continue circumnavigating the natural area, and link back to the trail you ran as you entered the natural area, retracing your steps.

STRETCHING

Although athletes have focused on flexibility for decades, coaches and trainers have only recently begun stressing the importance of stretching, although some discourage the practice.

Stretching used to be something smiling people wearing leotards did in black-and-white television programs while they bounced in what has become an antiquated school of ballistic stretching: "And one . . . two . . . three. . . ." Since those days, the art of stretching has grown dramatically, and trail runners may now choose between myriad techniques.

Stretching is fundamental to gaining and sustaining flexibility, which is a crucial element of trail running. By maintaining a regular stretching routine, trail runners are able to avoid injury by helping their muscles, tendons, and ligaments remain supple. Stretching staves off the stiffness and rigidity brought on by training and racing, and increases elasticity and resilience of connective tissues. Stretching also aids in recovery, injury prevention, stride length, strength, and nimbleness on the trail.

There is great diversity in stretching philosophies, and each school of thought has its own set of guidelines. The following recommendations for the trail runner were gleaned from an examination of these various approaches to stretching:

- Warm up before stretching. Warm muscles are less prone to strains, pulls, rips, or other injuries. Depending on the outside temperature, the location of the warm-up, the particular warm-up exercise, and its intensity, the prestretch period should equal approximately the time you would take to cover a flat mile. Do some stretching after the run to prevent postworkout soreness.

- Use proper form to isolate particular target muscles. If questions arise concerning how to go about a specific stretching routine, take a stretching class at a local health club or recreation center, consult with a personal trainer or coach, or check a book on stretching. Bob Anderson's 1975 book, *Stretching*, remains one of the better texts on the subject. Build a repertoire of stretches that addresses your particular needs, and stick to it as a regular part of your training schedule.

- Don't bounce. Ballistic stretching triggers a reflex that has the effect of tightening muscles. Ballistic stretching may also lead to a strain or other damage caused by bouncing beyond the natural range of motion. Using a long, sustained, static stretch after warming up releases tension that has built up in the area of focus.

- Isolate particular muscles that are the goal of a particular stretch, and "breathe" into specific muscles as you feel slow elongations of the targeted area. Stay relaxed and use slow rhythmic breathing. Hands, feet, shoulders, jaw, and face should not reflect tension.

- Continue the stretch to the point where a slight pull is felt, but not to the point of pain. According to Anderson, a mild comfortable stretch should result in tension that can be felt without pain. Do not gauge a stretch by how far you can reach; go by feel alone.

- If susceptible to particular types of injury, or if you are currently injured, pay special attention to stretching that area. In some cases, stretching may make the injury worse or prolong recovery. It may be worth consulting an expert before engaging in any stretching routine while injured.

- When performing a static pose, hold the stretch for as long as 30 seconds and stretch both sides equally. Anderson recommends that when doing a stretch, you should feel comfortable enough with the tension that the stretch can be held for 10 to 25 seconds, after which the initial feeling of the stretch should subside or disappear. That kind of stretching reduces muscle tension and maintains flexibility.

- To increase flexibility, Anderson recommends a "developmental stretch." After an easy stretch to the point where the feeling of tension dissipates, go into the pose again—but go deeper—until increased tension is felt. The stretch should not feel any more intense when held 10 to 30 seconds. If it does, ease off to a more comfortable position.

Incorporate the above rules as you customize a stretching routine that fits and appeals to your particular needs.

Consider incorporating some of the following stretches into your stretching regimen as a trail runner. These suggestions are by no means exhaustive, and it is recommended that additional resources be consulted to select and perfect an appropriate personal stretching routine.

Hamstrings: A modified hurdler's stretch involves sitting with one leg bent and that foot tucked against the inside of the thigh of the extended leg. From that position, lean forward (keeping the back straight) from the hips to touch with one or both hands the foot of the extended leg, reaching until tension is felt in the hamstring of the extended leg. Another hamstring stretch is to lie flat on your back, lift one leg and pull it toward the chest, with the other leg bent and its foot planted straight in front. A third hamstring stretch is to stand with one leg raised so that the foot rests on a solid object, such as a stool or a rock that is about at knee level. With the standing leg slightly bent, lean forward from the hips, keeping the back straight, and reach for the ankle of the extended leg until stretch is felt in the hamstring of the extended leg.

Iliotibial (IT) Band: The IT band stretches from just behind the hip, down the side of the leg, and connects to the top of the shin. When the IT band tightens, it can cause a flare-up on the side of the knee, resulting in pain. If a runner persists in running with a problematic IT band, it can ultimately seize up like an engine that has run dry of lubrication.

Any one—or all—of the following stretches can keep the IT band loose and flexible. In a sitting position with both legs stretched in front, cross one leg over the other and cradle the crossed leg in your arms, pulling the shin and foot of the crossed leg toward the chest until a stretch is felt in the hip of the bent leg. For a deeper stretch, cross the other leg over the extended leg, placing the foot of the bent leg on the other side of the extended leg, and place the opposite elbow against the bent knee (for example, if the left leg is bent, place the right elbow against the left side of the left knee), and press against the bent knee until the stretch is felt. Or, from a standing position, cross one leg in front of the other and lean forward to touch the toes until tension is felt in the hip of the rear leg. In the same pose, stand more upright and lean into the hip of the rear leg until tension is felt.

Groin: Because trail runners consistently have to dodge obstacles on the trail, they must incorporate considerably more lateral motion than do road runners. Sudden movement from side to side can lead to a pull or strain in the groin, unless that area is properly limber. One easy stretch is to sit down, pull both heels into the groin, and place the soles of both feet against each other, with knees close to or touching the ground. Increase the tension of the stretch by pulling the heels closer to the body, or lowering the knees to the ground by pressing elbows against knees.

Quadriceps: Descending a rocky trail at a fast pace places considerable stress on the quadriceps. A number of stretches can be performed to loosen your quads. One easy stretch is to stand on one foot and bend the other leg backward, reaching back with both hands to hold the foot of the bent leg, lifting the foot to the point where a stretch is felt. Another stretch is one that should not be performed by those with weak ankles or problem knees; if in doubt, consult an expert. Kneel on the ground with both knees, feet pointed backward and tucked underneath. Lean backward until the quads feel a stretch. Another basic quad exercise that helps build flexibility is to perform a static squat by slowly bending the knees while keeping the back straight and your weight centered over your pelvis.

Calves: Non-runners often chuckle at the sight of runners who appear to be trying to push over a building or lamppost. Little do the non-runners know that the runner is merely stretching calf muscles. This stretch involves standing about arm's length from a wall, post, tree, rock, or other fixed object and placing both hands against the object. Bend one leg off the ground as the other leg is stretched straight behind, keeping the heel of the straightened leg on the ground with the toes facing forward. Lean into the rear leg until that calf is stretched.

Devoting substantial time stretching calves may be well worth the investment, especially if focus is on the full range of the gastrocnemius muscles. Maintaining calf flexibility is very important for trail runners, who tend to run high on their toes or do a lot of hill work. For those limber enough to touch their toes, another way to stretch the calves is to sit on the ground and extend both legs parallel straight in front. Lean forward from the hips with the back straight and hold the toes, pulling them toward the body until a stretch is felt in the calves. If you cannot touch your toes, loop a band or towel around your toes, then pull on it to stretch the calves.

Ankles and Achilles Tendons: One of the greatest problem areas for trail runners is weak ankles. Maintaining flexible ankles helps prevent ankle rolls or sprains, and enables you to recover from what could be a calamity. Ankle rotations are easy to perform and can be done even while sitting. Lift one foot a few inches off the ground and slowly rotate it through its full range of motion. Rotate in both directions. To stretch the Achilles tendon, stand with one leg raised so that its heel rests on a solid object that is about at knee level. Lean forward, place both hands under the ball of your raised foot, and gradually pull toward the body. After feeling the stretch, point the toes toward the ground as far as possible.

Back and Trunk: Trail runners should invest heavily in a limber back and trunk. A tight back or midsection can lead to a nightmare of injuries, terrible running form, and an unhealthy posture. Practicing yoga on a regular basis can lead to a flexible back and relaxed running form. Back and trunk stretches include a standing waist twist, where hips are rotated in one direction as you look over your shoulder and hold the stretch, with hands on hips, knees slightly bent, and feet pointed forward. For a standing back extension stretch from the same standing position, place palms just above the hips with fingers pointing down, then slowly push the palms forward to create an extension in the lower back, and hold the stretch.

Another easy back stretch, which releases tension that may build up from running hills or rocky trails, is to lie on your back and bend your knees, lifting them slowly toward your chest until you can clasp your hands around the shins. Keep pulling the knees into the chest until the lower back feels stretched. An additional lower back stretch involves lying on your back with one leg extended flat on the ground. Bend the knee of the other leg and cross it over the extended leg, using the arm on the side of the extended leg to gently pull the bent knee down toward the ground, keeping both shoulders flat until a stretch is felt.

Upper Body: Because trail runners tend to use their arms more than road runners, due to the need for balance and occasional trail touchdowns or scrambling, it is more important to keep your arms loose. The same goes for a trail runner's neck and shoulders. Long ascents or descents can cause

trail runners to tense the upper body. The advantage of most upper body stretches is that they can be done on the fly, providing relief without the need to stop. If you grow tense during a run, try flapping your arms about wildly, throwing your head to and fro, and jutting your hips around in a very silly display. In addition to laughing at yourself—and encouraging anyone in sight to laugh as well—this odd behavior releases built-up stress, and at least temporarily realigns running form into a more relaxed and efficient posture.

To loosen tight shoulders and lower neck tension, incorporate slow-moving "windmills" (shoulder rotations with swinging arms) and exaggerated yawning-type movements in both directions. Rotate your head around in all directions, but be careful trying this on a run since it tends to momentarily compromise balance. For a more intense stretch, apply pressure on your head with your hands as the head is rotated. For good measure, throw in some shoulder shrugs, lifting the shoulders up toward the ears. To loosen arms and shoulders, raise one at a time, folding it at the elbow behind the head while using the other arm to gently apply pressure so that the hand of the bent arm flows down the upper back.

SOUTHEAST PORTLAND

MOUNT TABOR LOOP

THE RUN DOWN

START: Mount Tabor basketball court; elevation 561 feet

OVERALL DISTANCE: 2.9-mile loop

APPROXIMATE RUNNING TIME: 35 minutes

DIFFICULTY: Green

ELEVATION GAIN: 558 feet

PARKING: Parking lot and street parking are free

BEST SEASON TO RUN: Year-round

DOG FRIENDLY: Leashed dogs permitted

PARKING: Free

OTHER USERS: Bikers; no equestrians

CELL PHONE COVERAGE: Good

MORE INFORMATION: www .portlandoregon.gov/parks/ finder/index.cfm?PropertyID= 275&action=ViewPark

FINDING THE TRAILHEAD

From SE 60th Avenue, turn east on SE Salmon, which becomes SE Reservoir Road Drive where the road enters the park. There is parking all along the roadway, as well as in a lot on the left-hand side of the road about a quarter-mile into the park. There are restrooms at this location. Start your run at the Mount Tabor Park basketball court.

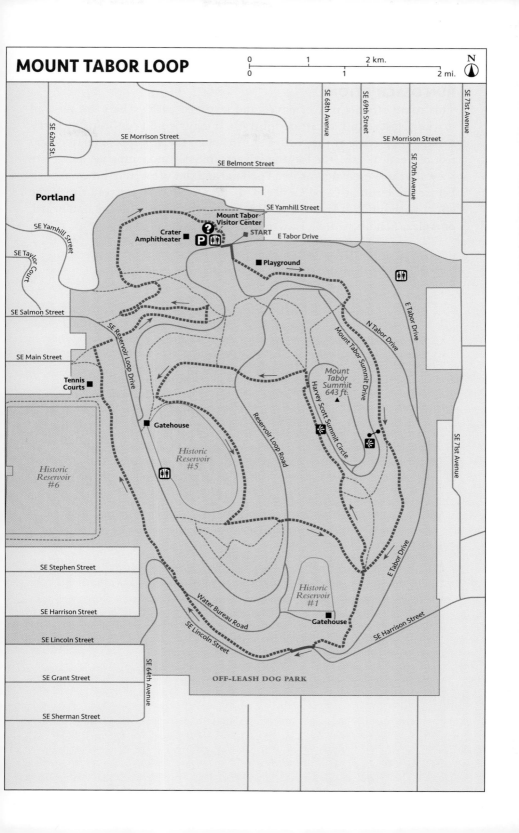

RUN DESCRIPTION

This route offers a mix of paved and unpaved paths. There are no trail markers, just color indications for trails. It may be a bit confusing, so carry a map or a picture of the park area. Although there is approximately 600 feet of vertical gain, the footing is very smooth and runnable. There are views to the west of downtown Portland and the West Hills. Enjoy a snack before your run at Good Coffee, 4747 SE Division Street, and finish the effort with lunch at Hawthorne Hophouse, 4111 SE Hawthorne Boulevard, or Apizza Scholls, 4741 SE Hawthorne Boulevard.

POWELL BUTTE NATURE PARK 4.4-MILE LOOP

Opened to the public in 1990, the mix of terrain in Powell Butte Nature Park's 608 acres includes open meadows with fantastic views of Cascade mountain peaks, with Mount Hood (on a clear day) to the east, Mount Saint Helens and Mount Adams to the north, and Mount Jefferson to the southeast. Douglas fir abounds within the canopied forest along the single-track trails, as well.

THE RUN DOWN

START: On the Mountain View Trail; elevation 463 feet

OVERALL DISTANCE: 4.4-mile loop

APPROXIMATE RUNNING TIME: 50 minutes

DIFFICULTY: Green

ELEVATION GAIN: 658 feet

BEST SEASON TO RUN: Year-round, although the singletrack can get a bit muddy in heavy rains

DOG FRIENDLY: Leashed dogs permitted

PARKING: Free

OTHER USERS: Mountain bikers and equestrians on designated trails

CELL PHONE COVERAGE: Good

MORE INFORMATION: www .portlandoregon.gov/parks/ finder/index.cfm?action=View Park&PropertyID=528

FINDING THE TRAILHEAD

The park is located at 16160 SE Powell Boulevard. From the parking lot, the trailhead is just a short walk uphill on pavement. There are restrooms near the trailhead.

POWELL BUTTE NATURE PARK 4.4-MILE LOOP

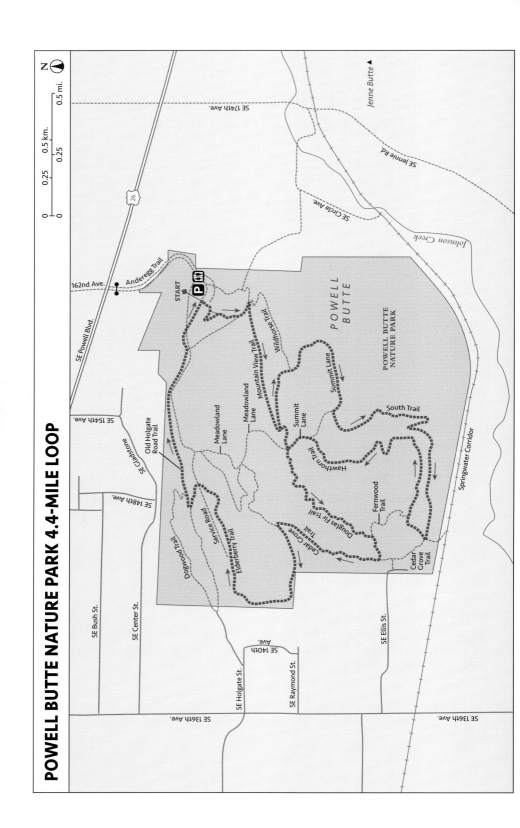

RUN DESCRIPTION

Heading out on a packed gravel pathway, go in a clockwise direction on the Mountain View Trail, connecting with the Cedar Grove Trail, which links to the Elderberry Trail. In the upper reaches of the park, the Holgate Lane connects with the Dogwood Trail for a bit of a dogleg section that connects back to the Holgate Lane and the Pipeline Lane to close the loop back at the visitor center. You'll experience a variety of surfaces and terrain running in and out of the forest on singletrack, including wide pathways, packed gravel, and even some well-maintained steps. Enjoy coffee postrun at Dutch Bros., 13640 SE Division Street.

POWELL BUTTE PERIMETER LOOP

THE RUN DOWN

START: On the Mountain View Trail; elevation 463 feet

OVERALL DISTANCE: 5.5-mile loop

APPROXIMATE RUNNING TIME: 70 minutes

DIFFICULTY: Blue

ELEVATION GAIN: 712 feet

BEST SEASON TO RUN: Year-round, but trails can be muddy in the rainy season

DOG FRIENDLY: Leashed dogs permitted

PARKING: Free

OTHER USERS: Mountain bikers, equestrians

CELL PHONE COVERAGE: Good

MORE INFORMATION: www .portlandoregon.gov/parks/ finder/index.cfm?action=View Park&PropertyID=528

FINDING THE TRAILHEAD

The park is located at 16160 SE Powell Boulevard. From the parking lot, the trailhead is just a short walk uphill on pavement. There are restrooms near the trailhead.

RUN DESCRIPTION

Run this very obvious route in a clockwise direction, starting at the trailhead near the interpretive center. You'll experience singletrack trail, wide gravel pathways, forested terrain, and some roots and rocks. Views abound on a clear day.

POWELL BUTTE NATURE PARK PERIMETER LOOP

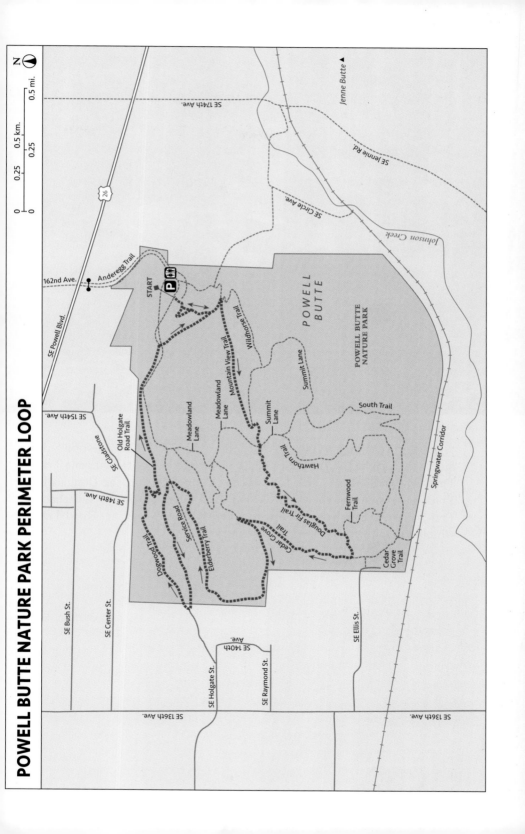

Leave the parking area on the Mountain View Trail. Turn left on Summit Lane; turn left on the South Trail; turn right on the Hawthorne Trail. Turn left on Summit Lane, followed by a quick left on the Douglas Fir Trail. Turn right on the Cedar Grove Trail; turn left on the Elderberry Trail; turn right on Holgate Lane to where it joins the Service Road Trail, which will take you back to the parking area.

TRAIL SURFACES:
MUD, SNOW, AND ICE

No Portland trail running guide worth its salt would neglect to address mud running, given its prominence. The best way to deal with mud on the trail is to enjoy it, and to get as dirty as possible early in the run so you won't worry about it thereafter. Soft mud enables a lower impact run, especially on the descents, where mud provides a great surface for slowing the pace without stressing joints.

To avoid slipping, it may help to shorten your stride, run more upright than normal, and keep your elbows more angled for lateral balance. If you begin to slip, try to relax and control the recovery so as not to overreact and fall in the opposite direction.

If water is running down the trail, the best bet is to run where water is moving most rapidly because that surface will probably be the most firm. A faster current tends to remove most of the sticky sediment, leaving behind gravel and rock. Although the runner will get wet, the likelihood of getting bogged down in muddier trail borders is markedly decreased. This technique is also friendlier to the trail because of the lower environmental impact.

From an environmental standpoint, resist the temptation to run alongside the trail in an effort to avoid getting muddy. Submitting to the temptation leads to wider trails; and if everyone did it, pathways would soon be major thruways instead of singletrack trails. Typical Portland metropolitan area weather causes muddy trails and, depending on the sensitivity of the specific trail system, it may be advisable to avoid certain trails until they have a chance to dry.

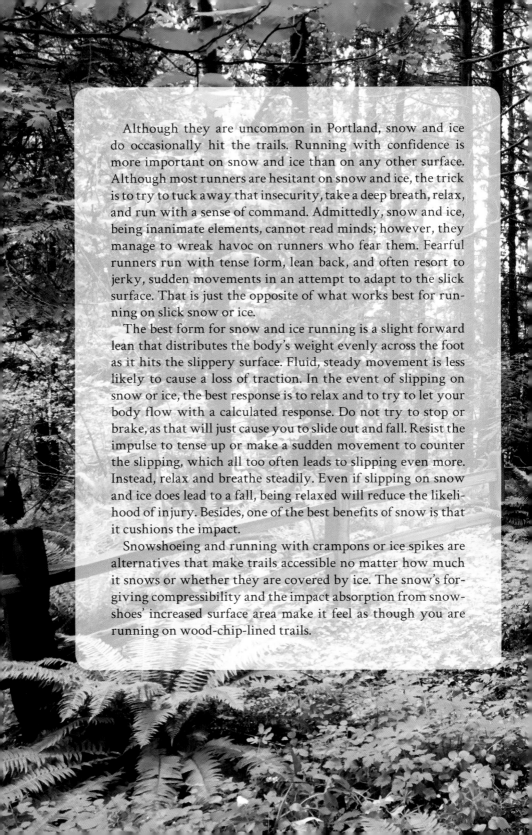

Although they are uncommon in Portland, snow and ice do occasionally hit the trails. Running with confidence is more important on snow and ice than on any other surface. Although most runners are hesitant on snow and ice, the trick is to try to tuck away that insecurity, take a deep breath, relax, and run with a sense of command. Admittedly, snow and ice, being inanimate elements, cannot read minds; however, they manage to wreak havoc on runners who fear them. Fearful runners run with tense form, lean back, and often resort to jerky, sudden movements in an attempt to adapt to the slick surface. That is just the opposite of what works best for running on slick snow or ice.

The best form for snow and ice running is a slight forward lean that distributes the body's weight evenly across the foot as it hits the slippery surface. Fluid, steady movement is less likely to cause a loss of traction. In the event of slipping on snow or ice, the best response is to relax and to try to let your body flow with a calculated response. Do not try to stop or brake, as that will just cause you to slide out and fall. Resist the impulse to tense up or make a sudden movement to counter the slipping, which all too often leads to slipping even more. Instead, relax and breathe steadily. Even if slipping on snow and ice does lead to a fall, being relaxed will reduce the likelihood of injury. Besides, one of the best benefits of snow is that it cushions the impact.

Snowshoeing and running with crampons or ice spikes are alternatives that make trails accessible no matter how much it snows or whether they are covered by ice. The snow's forgiving compressibility and the impact absorption from snowshoes' increased surface area make it feel as though you are running on wood-chip-lined trails.

SOUTHWEST PORTLAND

COUNCIL CREST TRAIL (4T TRAIL)

THE RUN DOWN

START: South Waterfront Lower Tram Terminal; elevation 72 feet

OVERALL DISTANCE: 6.6 miles

APPROXIMATE RUNNING TIME: 2 hours (depending on transportation schedules)

DIFFICULTY: Blue

ELEVATION GAIN: 1,322 feet

BEST SEASON TO RUN: Year-round

DOG FRIENDLY: Leashed dogs permitted

PARKING: Free

OTHER USERS: None

CELL PHONE COVERAGE: Good

MORE INFORMATION: https://4ttrail.wordpress.com/

FINDING THE TRAILHEAD

Start at the South Waterfront Lower Tram Terminal, located on SW Moody Avenue next to the Oregon Health and Sciences University building (OHSU).

RUN DESCRIPTION

This route has it all—"Trail, Tram, Trolley, Train"—resulting in the aptly named 4T Trail. From the start at the lower tram station, you will experience the trails in and out of the forest, public transportation, roads, stairs, and views of Mount Hood. The entire route is very well signed,

COUNCIL CREST TRAIL (4T TRAIL)

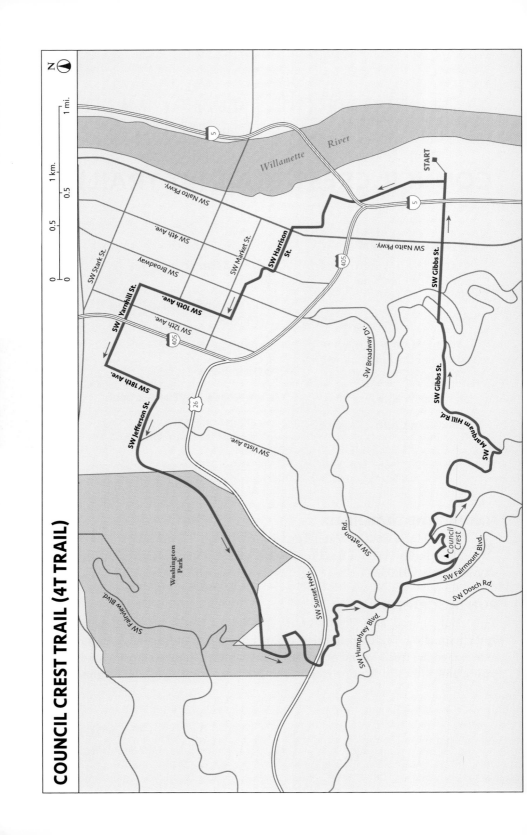

with 4T trail markers pointing the way through the neighborhood and other sections. The route ends at the upper tram station. Tram rides down are free. Some options for sustenance along the way include the Daily Cafe at the Tram, 3355 SW Bond Avenue, and the Little Big Burger, 3704 SW Bond Avenue.

OUT-AND-BACK KEYHOLE WITH A VIEW

Located in Forest Park, 178-acre Marquam Nature Park is comprised primarily of singletrack trails within canopied forest. Be mindful of falling tree limbs on the trails in early spring. This is common in many forested areas in the Pacific Northwest, when the weight of water absorbed during the rainy season tends to put stress on branches and causes breakage. Trails are well marked. This is also the trail portion of the 4T Portland experience—Trail, Tram, Trolley, Train.

THE RUN DOWN

START: Marquam Park Shelter; elevation 316 feet

OVERALL DISTANCE: 3 miles out and back (on a parallel trail)

APPROXIMATE RUNNING TIME: 40 minutes

DIFFICULTY: Blue due to the elevation gain

ELEVATION GAIN: 761 feet

BEST SEASON TO RUN: Year-round

DOG FRIENDLY: Leashed pets permitted

PARKING: Free

OTHER USERS: Foot traffic. Can be crowded, and sightings of local running celebrities are common

CELL PHONE COVERAGE: Very good

MORE INFORMATION: www .fmnp.org

FINDING THE TRAILHEAD

Park in the lot at SW Marquam Street and Sam Jackson Park Road, located a short walk from the trailhead (fifteen spots). You can also park at the nearby Duniway Track and run about 1 mile for a warm-up to the trail.

OUT-AND-BACK KEYHOLE WITH A VIEW

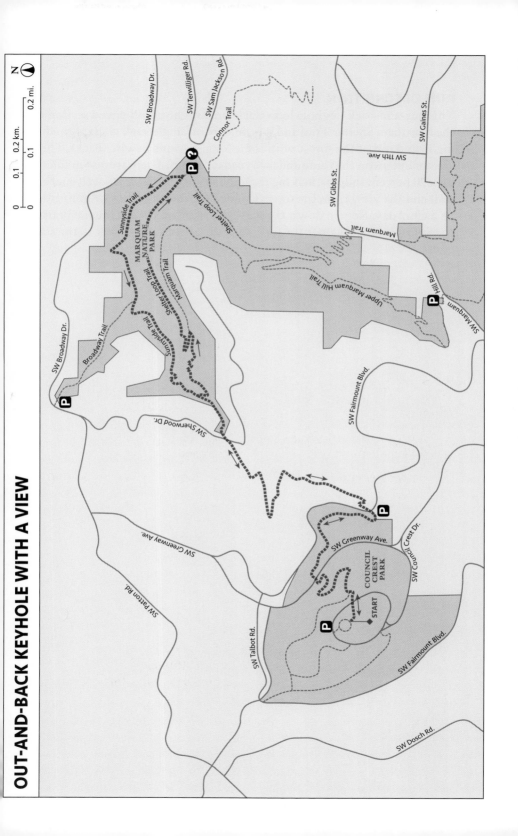

RUN DESCRIPTION

This out-and-back keyhole loop starts on a slight uphill paved section on the Marquam Shelter Trail and is primarily on singletrack trails, meandering in and out of the forest with some long, sweeping switchbacks. There are some steps on the route and two road crossings. There are also gradients over 20 percent in spots, making for some steep running. It is a well-marked trail and the view from the top at Council Crest will include Mount Hood on a clear day. Return down the way you came on the Marquam Trail to the Sunnyside Trail, or at the fork, take the Shelter Trail back to the start point.

MARQUAM NATURE PARK 4.5-MILE LOOP

THE RUN DOWN

START: Uphill from the parking lot on SW Marquam St.; elevation 988 feet

OVERALL DISTANCE: 4.5-mile loop

APPROXIMATE RUNNING TIME: 50 minutes

DIFFICULTY: Blue

ELEVATION GAIN: 988 feet

BEST SEASON TO RUN: Year-round although the singletrack can get a bit muddy in heavy rains

DOG FRIENDLY: Leashed dogs permitted

PARKING: Free

OTHER USERS: None

CELL PHONE COVERAGE: Good

MORE INFORMATION: www.fmnp.org

PORTLAND

FINDING THE TRAILHEAD

Take SW Marquam Street off Sam Jackson Park Road. Approximately 100 yards down SW Marquam Street, there is signage on the right-hand side for Marquam Nature Park. The trailhead is located uphill from the parking lot.

RUN DESCRIPTION

There are three trail options from this location. Continue uphill on Marquam Street, which dead-ends to a gate. You can continue uphill on the Shelter Trail, which is located immediately beyond the bollards and provides a loop route experience. Additionally, there are two singletrack trails: One is the Sunnyside Trail, to the right, and the other is the other end of the Shelter Trail.

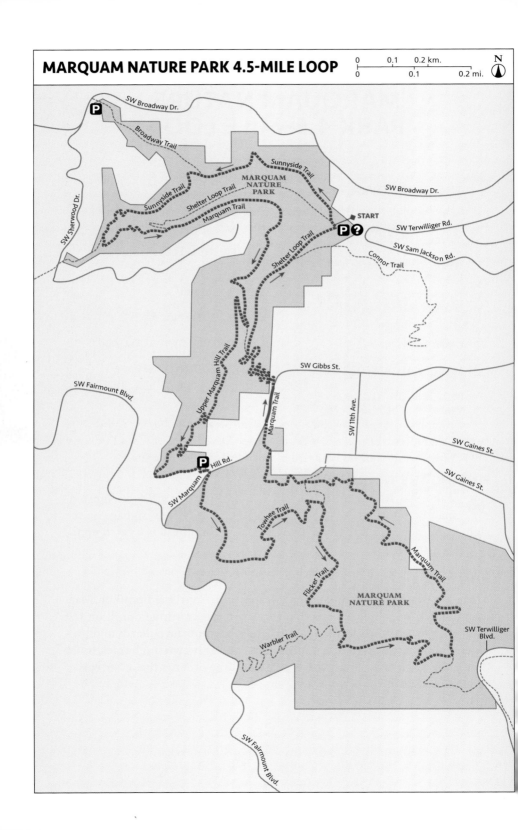

MARQUAM NATURE PARK 4.5-MILE LOOP

0   0.1   0.2 km.
0   0.1   0.2 mi.

N

SW Broadway Dr.

Broadway Trail

Sunnyside Trail

Sunnyside Trail

SW Broadway Dr.

MARQUAM
NATURE
PARK

Shelter Loop Trail

SW Sherwood Dr.

Marquam Trail

START

SW Terwilliger Rd.

SW Sam Jackson Rd.

Shelter Loop Trail

Connor Trail

SW Gibbs St.

SW Fairmount Blvd

Upper Marquam Hill Trail

Marquam Trail

SW 11th Ave.

SW Gaines St.

Hill Rd.

SW Gaines St.

SW Marquam

Towhee Trail

Marquam Trail

Flicket Trail

MARQUAM
NATURE
PARK

SW Terwilliger
Blvd.

Warbler Trail

SW Fairmount Blvd.

Following the run, enjoy some food and drink at spots such as the Stumptown Coffee Roasters, 1026 SW Stark Street; Deschutes Brewery Portland, 210 NW 11th Avenue; and Lair Hill Bistro, 2823 SW 1st Avenue.

WILDWOOD TRAIL END-TO-END

THE RUN DOWN

START: Oregon Zoo; elevation 883 feet

OVERALL DISTANCE: 30 miles one way

APPROXIMATE RUNNING TIME: 5 to 12 hours

DIFFICULTY: Black for distance; blue for trails

ELEVATION GAIN: 3,530 feet

BEST SEASON TO RUN: Year-round

DOG FRIENDLY: Leashed dogs permitted

PARKING: Free

OTHER USERS: Mountain bikers and equestrians on designated trails

CELL PHONE COVERAGE: Good

MORE INFORMATION: www .forestparkconservancy.org

FINDING THE TRAILHEAD

 Start at the Oregon Zoo at mile zero and end at Newberry Road; or turn around at any point for an out-and-back effort.

RUN DESCRIPTION

This well-maintained, buffed-out singletrack traverses terrain in the forest. There are three road crossings if the route is done in its entirety. The trail stretches across the largest urban forest in the United States, Portland's 5,000-acre Forest Park.

WILDWOOD TRAIL END-TO-END

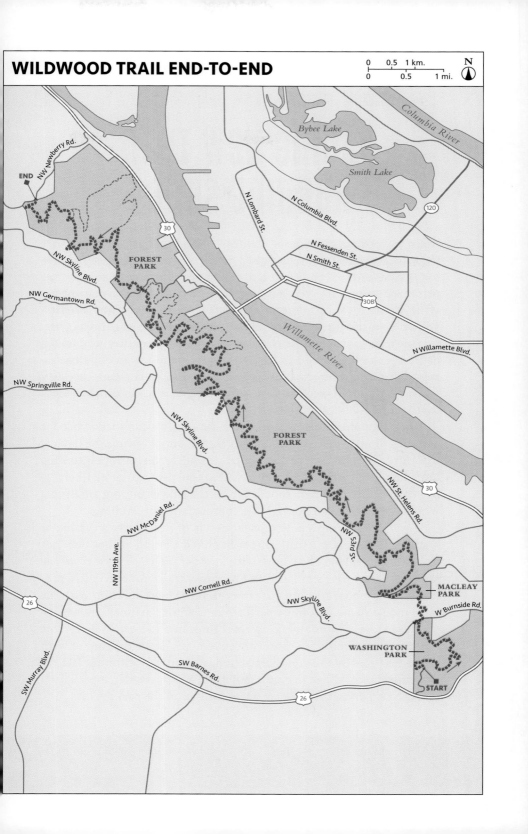

BUYING NEW TRAIL-RUNNING SHOES

Begin by looking at the wear and tear on your old, "spent" shoes. Are the soles worn in certain parts and not in others? Wear patterns provide evidence of overpronation or supination. By looking at wet footprints left after a shower, bath, or swim and comparing your prints with others, you can determine relative arch height and forefoot width. Armed with those particular "foot notes," a trail runner is better able to shop for shoes at a local specialty running store, in a catalog, or from an online vendor, and better prepared to ask an expert salesperson for a recommendation. It is best to go to a running specialty store, where a foot specialist can perform a gait analysis using a videotaped treadmill or other test.

When shopping for trail shoes, wear the same kind of socks worn for running. Similarly, those who use orthotics should bring the devices to ensure shoes fit once the orthotic is inserted. Also, it is best to shop immediately or soon after a run, when your feet are most likely to be swollen. Ultrarunners should err on the side of buying a half to a whole size larger than normal to accommodate foot swelling.

Be wary of buying a new model or style of shoes from a catalog or website. Just because a trail runner has liked a brand of shoe does not mean the runner will be happy with another model or style from the same manufacturer. Similarly, just because a trail runner enjoys a particular shoe model does not guarantee that the next iteration with the same model name will fit or perform in a similar manner. Shoe manufacturers are always tweaking their lines in an effort to better the product, and all too often those "improvements" leave the runner with a shoe that goes by the same name but has an entirely different feel, fit, or performance. When in doubt, buy from a local retailer, especially if you can test-drive the shoes on a treadmill or in the parking lot.

GOOSE HOLLOW TO ZOO HILL CLIMB

THE RUN DOWN

START: Goose Hollow Inn; elevation 180 feet

OVERALL DISTANCE: 4.4 miles one way

APPROXIMATE RUNNING TIME: 70 minutes

DIFFICULTY: Blue

ELEVATION GAIN: 942 feet

BEST SEASON TO RUN: Year-round

DOG FRIENDLY: Leashed dogs permitted

PARKING: Free

OTHER USERS: Cyclists

CELL PHONE COVERAGE: Good

MORE INFORMATION: http:// explorewashingtonpark.org

FINDING THE TRAILHEAD

Start at Goose Hollow Inn, located at 1927 SW Jefferson Street. Parking is available at the trailhead. Head west along SW Jefferson Street under the historic Vista Avenue Bridge.

RUN DESCRIPTION

This route is great for uphill intervals or a lung-busting uphill tempo run. Start on the entrance to Washington Park on SW Jefferson Street, and go up the paved Madison Trail in Washington Park, to the Mac Trail just beneath the International Test Rose Garden, and climb the Mac Trail all the way up to the Zoo/MAX Train stop, which is also the start of the Wildwood Trail. When heading uphill, cross several roadways on the

GOOSE HOLLOW TO ZOO HILL CLIMB

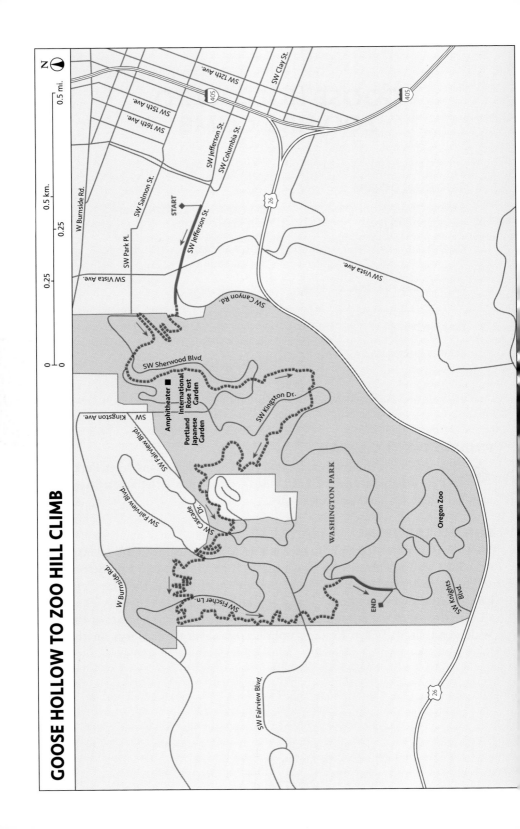

winding trails. To avoid the downhill run, ride four minutes back down to the trailhead on the MAX train. Enjoy eats at Coffeehouse Northwest, 1951 W Burnside Street; dine at your starting point at Goose Hollow Inn, or at Laughing Planet Cafe, 1755 SW Jefferson Street.

TRYON CREEK 1.2-MILE

With 8 miles of trails over 658 acres, Tryon Creek State Natural Area is Oregon's only state park within a major metropolitan area. The park is located off I-5 at Terwilliger Boulevard in Southwest Portland. The nearest bus routes are the #39 and #35. A mixture of singletrack and wide pathways crisscross the park. Carrying a map (a photo on your smartphone) would be beneficial to better navigate routes due to multiple trail connectors and intersections. It is better to look like a tourist than to be lost.

THE RUN DOWN

START: Near the visitor center; elevation 252 feet

OVERALL DISTANCE: 1.2-mile loop

APPROXIMATE RUNNING TIME: 15 minutes

DIFFICULTY: Green

ELEVATION GAIN: 166 feet

BEST SEASON TO RUN: During heavy rains this can be a bit muddy, but the trail has very good absorption due to hard-packed dirt

DOG FRIENDLY: Leashed dogs permitted

PARKING: Free

OTHER USERS: Equestrians on designated trails; mountain bikers on paved trails only

CELL PHONE COVERAGE: Very good

MORE INFORMATION: http://oregonstateparks.org/index.cfm?do=parkPage.dsp_parkPage&parkId=103

FINDING THE TRAILHEAD

Parking is located at 11321 SW Terwilliger Boulevard, and there is also on-street parking with a short walk to the trails. Know that this is a very busy venue on the weekends. The trailhead is near the visitor center, with signage indicating the various trails accessed from this point.

TRYON CREEK 1.2-MILE

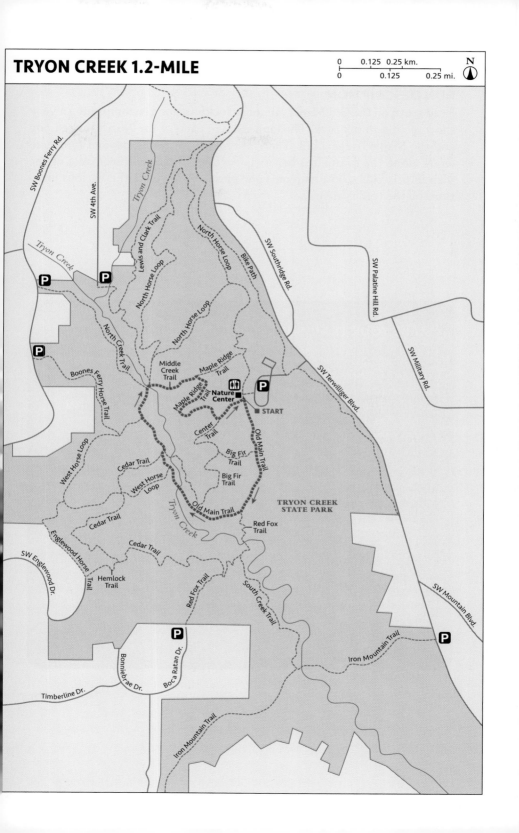

RUN DESCRIPTION

Head south on the Old Man Trail for a clockwise loop encompassing a very short section in the park. The loop takes in parts of the North Horse Loop and the Maple Ridge Trail. There are foot bridges to cross and forests to enjoy along the route. It is beneficial to carry a map, a screen shot of the map in this guide, or a map on your phone to navigate the various junctions on the trail system.

MAKE YOUR TRAIL SHOES LAST LONGER

The best way to prolong the life of trail shoes is to have several pairs and rotate them so that one pair is never used for more than a couple of consecutive runs without getting a rest. Using old beater pairs on days when the weather is particularly "sucky" also extends the life of newer shoes that you would rather not expose to brutal conditions. Like allowing the body to have recovery days, giving shoes some time off allows the midsole materials—the parts that usually break down the fastest—to decompress between runs.

It is a good idea to wash shoes by wiping them down to remove caked mud. Remove the insole inserts from the footbeds and insert balled-up newspaper in each footbed while the shoes dry at room temperature. If the shoes are soaked, it may be necessary to replace the newspaper once or twice.

It is best to allow shoes to dry slowly. That way they will be less likely to delaminate. Do not run the shoes through the washing machine or dryer or put them in the oven, as this can damage the midsole material. Reserve your favorite trail shoes for the activity they were made for: Do not wear them to work, for walking, or for hiking because that compresses and stresses them in ways that are not conducive to running—plus, such activities break them down prematurely.

TRYON CREEK 3.4-MILE

THE RUN DOWN

START: Near the interpretive center; elevation 312 feet

OVERALL DISTANCE: 3.4-mile loop

APPROXIMATE RUNNING TIME: 40 minutes

DIFFICULTY: Green

ELEVATION GAIN: 397 feet

BEST SEASON TO RUN: During heavy rains this can be a bit muddy, but the trail has very good absorption due to hard-packed dirt

DOG FRIENDLY: Leashed dogs permitted

PARKING: Free

OTHER USERS: Equestrians on designated trails; mountain bikers on paved trails only

CELL PHONE COVERAGE: Good

MORE INFORMATION: http://oregonstateparks.org/index.cfm?do=parkPage.dsp_parkPage&parkId=103

FINDING THE TRAILHEAD

Proceed to the entrance off SW Terwilliger Boulevard, which is indicated by signage stating TRYON CREEK STATE PARK NATURE STORE. Park in the lot just west of SW Terwilliger Boulevard. Proceed to the trailhead signage near the interpretive center. There are restrooms at the center, as well as a drinking fountain.

RUN DESCRIPTION

This loop is run in a counterclockwise direction. You'll enjoy smooth surfaces throughout the run, along with a smattering of exposed tree roots and rocks on the trails. The trails are well maintained and not technical. There is a very informative sign at the Nature Center with a great map. Take a photo when you start to plan your route. All creek crossings have footbridges.

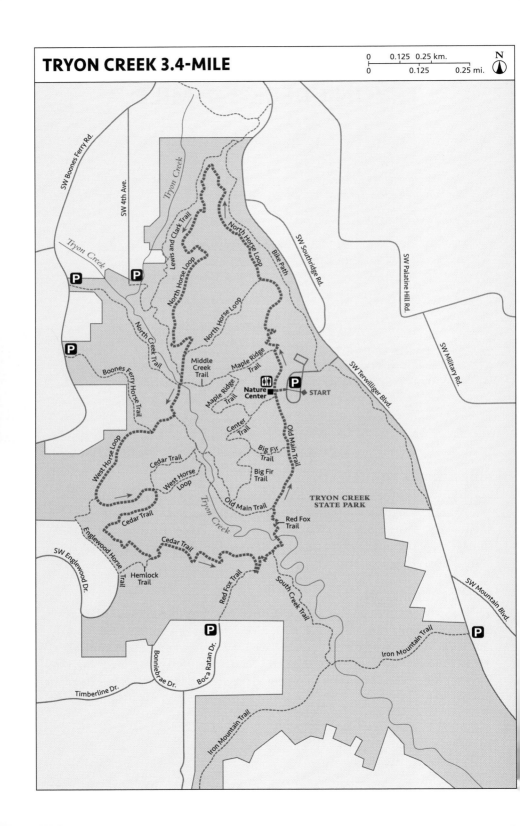

TRYON CREEK 3.4-MILE

0   0.125 0.25 km.

0   0.125   0.25 mi.

N

SW Boones Ferry Rd.

SW 4th Ave.

Tryon Creek

Tryon Creek

Tryon Creek

Lewis and Clark Trail

North Horse Loop

North Horse Loop

North Horse Loop

Bike Path

SW Southridge Rd.

SW Palatine Hill Rd.

SW Military Rd.

North Creek Trail

Boones Ferry Horse Trail

Middle Creek Trail

Maple Ridge Trail

Maple Ridge Trail

Nature Center

START

SW Terwilliger Blvd.

West Horse Loop

Cedar Trail

West Horse Loop

Center Trail

Big Fir Trail

Big Fir Trail

Old Main Trail

Cedar Trail

Old Main Trail

Red Fox Trail

TRYON CREEK STATE PARK

Englewood Horse Trail

SW Englewood Dr.

Cedar Trail

Hemlock Trail

Red Fox Trail

South Creek Trail

Bonniebrae Dr.

Boca Ratan Dr.

Timberline Dr.

Iron Mountain Trail

Iron Mountain Trail

SW Mountain Blvd.

Starting on the North Horse Loop, connect to the West Horse Loop after approximately 1.3 miles. Follow West Horse Loop less than 1 mile to the intersection with the Cedar Trail. At just under 3 miles, connect to the Old Man Trail, which heads back to the starting point.

TRYON CREEK PERIMETER LOOP

THE RUN DOWN

START: Near the interpretive center; elevation 331 feet

OVERALL DISTANCE: 4.5-mile loop

APPROXIMATE RUNNING TIME: 50 minutes

DIFFICULTY: Blue

ELEVATION GAIN: 459 feet

BEST SEASON TO RUN: During heavy rains this can be a bit muddy, but the trail has very good absorption due to hard-packed dirt

DOG FRIENDLY: Leashed dogs permitted

PARKING: Free

OTHER USERS: Equestrians on designated trails; mountain bikers on paved trails only

CELL PHONE COVERAGE: Good

MORE INFORMATION: http://oregonstateparks.org/index.cfm?do=parkPage.dsp_parkPage&parkId=103

FINDING THE TRAILHEAD

Proceed to the entrance off SW Terwilliger Boulevard, which is indicated by signage stating TRYON CREEK STATE PARK NATURE STORE. Park in the lot just west of SW Terwilliger Boulevard. Proceed to the trailhead signage near the interpretive center. There are restrooms at the center, as well as a drinking fountain.

RUN DESCRIPTION

Start on the Terwilliger Trail, heading south approximately 0.8 mile to the Iron Mountain Trail. Run east on this section for approximately 0.5 mile to

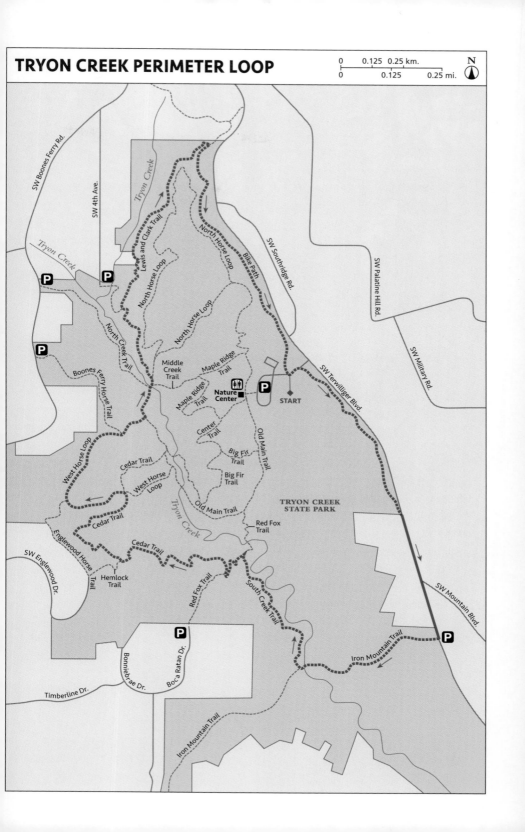

TRYON CREEK PERIMETER LOOP

0   0.125   0.25 km.
0   0.125   0.25 mi.

N

SW Boones Ferry Rd.

SW 4th Ave.

Tryon Creek

Tryon Creek

P

P

P

P

Lewis and Clark Trail

North Horse Loop

North Horse Loop

North Horse Loop

Bike Path

SW Southridge Rd.

SW Terwilliger Blvd.

SW Palatine Hill Rd.

SW Military Rd.

North Creek Trail

Boones Ferry Horse Trail

Middle Creek Trail

Maple Ridge Trail

Maple Ridge Trail

Nature Center

START

P

Center Trail

Big Fir Trail

Big Fir Trail

Old Main Trail

West Horse Loop

Cedar Trail

West Horse Loop

Old Main Trail

Red Fox Trail

TRYON CREEK STATE PARK

Tryon Creek

Englewood Horse Trail

SW Englewood Dr.

Cedar Trail

Cedar Trail

Hemlock Trail

Red Fox Trail

South Creek Trail

SW Mountain Blvd.

P

P

Iron Mountain Trail

Iron Mountain Trail

Bonniebrae Dr.

Boca Ratan Dr.

Timberline Dr.

Iron Mountain Trail

the South Creek Trail, which becomes the Cedar Trail after crossing over the Red Fox Trail. After 2.4 miles, reach the junction with the West Horse Loop Trail and continue to the Lewis and Clark Trail at approximately 3 miles. At just under 4 miles, turn south on the Terwilliger Trail back to the starting point.

TUALATIN RIVER AND FANNO CREEK 5.8-MILE

THE RUN DOWN

START: Near the dog park in Tualatin Community Park; elevation 112 feet

OVERALL DISTANCE: 5.8 miles in two loops

APPROXIMATE RUNNING TIME: 70 minutes

DIFFICULTY: Green

ELEVATION GAIN: 328 feet

BEST SEASON TO RUN: Year-round

DOG FRIENDLY: Leashed dogs permitted

PARKING: Free

OTHER USERS: Cyclists

CELL PHONE COVERAGE: Good

MORE INFORMATION: www .oregonhikers.org/field_guide/ Cook_and_Durham_City_ Parks_Hike

FINDING THE TRAILHEAD

Start at the Tualatin Community Park, 8515 SW Tualatin Road, in Tualatin. This park has ball fields, tennis courts, a dog park, and several parking areas. The trail is on the north side of the parking lot near the dog park. Walk north past the skate park, baseball diamond, and basketball court to start your run near the dog park.

RUN DESCRIPTION

This route is flat as a pancake. It's great for beginners or for those wanting to do a short and fast tempo run or pickups. Run along the Tualatin River and Fanno Creek, through wetlands, and through three city parks on a mixture of paved paths and trails, enjoying a wild paradise in the middle of suburbia. The main Fanno Creek Trail and the Tualatin River Trail are named and marked, but many smaller feeder trails are not.

From the SW Tualatin Road entrance, run east, toward the river, circumnavigating the park in the counterclockwise direction. Follow the Tualatin River Greenway path to the north, along the riverbank, crossing

TUALATIN RIVER AND FANNO CREEK 5.8-MILE

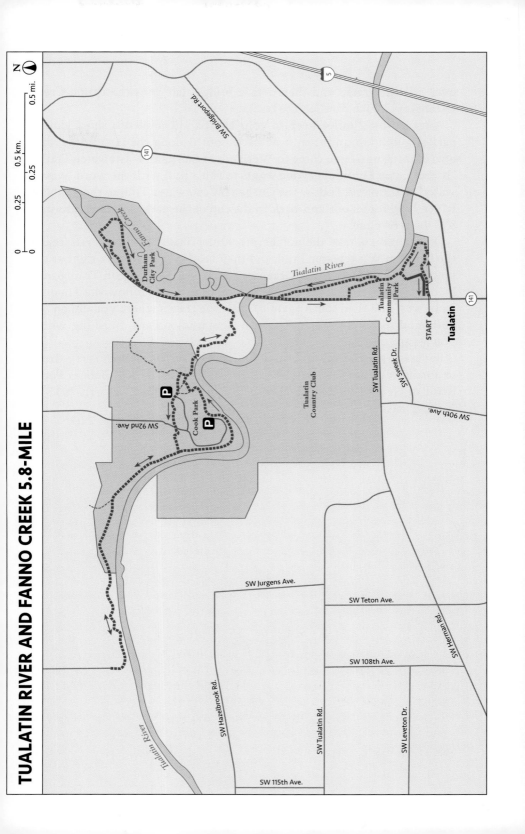

over railroad tracks and then over a bridge that joins the Fanno Creek Greenway, which parallels the tracks.

After almost 2 miles, keep to your right and complete a short loop as part of a lollipop, and then head back (south) along the same route for a quarter mile until you come to Wetlands at Durham Wastewater Trail . . . because, you know, everyone wants to run a trail with the word "wastewater" in the name. Follow the Durham Wastewater Trail to the Tualatin River Trail for an out-and-back to the end of the park, where it runs into SW 108th Avenue.

On the return, take the northern route of Tualatin River Trail, rejoin the Durham Wastewater Trail, and then head south, taking a right at the juncture with Fanno Creek Greenway. Keep on the Tonquin Trail, paralleling the train tracks, to your second left, where you follow the Tonquin Trail west and then south again to cross the tracks where you did on the outbound route. Return to Tualatin Community Park, finishing where you began.

Be sure to stop for eats at Doughnut Land, 19350 SW Boones Ferry Road, or for more substantial eats at C I Bar & Grill, 18786 SW Boones Ferry Road, or New Seasons Market, Nyberg Rivers Shopping Center, 7703 SW Nyberg Street.

CROSS-TRAINING

Trail runners are often well-rounded athletes who enjoy a fine collection of outdoor endurance activities. With the changing seasons, trail runners are likely to supplement their recreational routines with Alpine and Nordic skiing; snowshoeing; kayaking; swimming; pool running; climbing; hiking; walking; martial arts; dance; horseback riding; skating; mountain, road, and stationary biking; and other pursuits. Engaging in other sports helps balance a trail runner's training regimen, develop supporting muscles, and condition the cardio system, and throws an element of excitement and vivaciousness into the mix. Because running is not necessarily a full-body sport, integrating other activities into training helps strengthen the trunk and upper body, which might otherwise grow weak from neglect.

Skills and strengths gained from cross-training easily translate to trail running. The limbering and strengthening of muscles that comes from rock climbing, the lung capacity gained from Nordic skiing, high altitude training from mountaineering, descending skills from mountain biking, the leg strength gained from snowshoeing, the muscular balance gained from swimming—all of these make for a better trail runner.

Cross-training also gives some perspective to trail running. Cross-training can be used as "active rest"; you can feel good about not running while pursuing another discipline or developing new skills that enhance the trail-running dimension. By becoming passionate about other athletic endeavors, a trail runner is more likely to take adequate time away from running when a recovery period is necessary to recuperate from an overuse injury or to avoid overuse. Knowing there are alternatives to running trails certainly helps during a time of injury, boredom, or burnout from running.

Cross-training is easily integrated into the trail-running routine by substituting a different discipline for a running session or two each week. These cross-training sessions should be of equivalent intensity as the running would have been, as measured by heart rate, effort, and time. For example, after a long trail run on Sunday, replace the normal 45-minute Monday recovery run with a 45-minute swim, bike, or Nordic ski session of equivalent effort.

Depending on your trail-running goals, cross-training should complement and supplement running, but not supplant it. Although cross-training is an excellent way to maintain fitness while giving running muscles some time off, cross-training should be thought of as active rest, in that it should not be so strenuous or depleting that you are too exhausted to pursue trail-running training. Exercise some caution when trying a new sport, because it is easy to strain muscles that are not trained for that specific activity. It is rather disappointing to spoil your trail-running training effort because of an injury resulting from a cross-training mishap.

NORTHWEST PORTLAND

SALTZMAN 4-MILE LOOP

THE RUN DOWN

START: End of NW Saltzman Rd.; elevation 394 feet

OVERALL DISTANCE: 3.9-mile loop

APPROXIMATE RUNNING TIME: 45 minutes

DIFFICULTY: Blue

ELEVATION GAIN: 719 feet

BEST SEASON TO RUN: Year-round

DOG FRIENDLY: Leashed dogs permitted

PARKING: Free

OTHER USERS: Cyclists

CELL PHONE COVERAGE: Good

MORE INFORMATION: www .forestparkconservancy.org

FINDING THE TRAILHEAD

If taking public transportation, take the #16 bus toward Sauvie Island and get off at the NW St. Helens and Saltzman stop. Run up NW Saltzman Road to the trailhead. You can also drive northwest out of Portland on NW St. Helens Road. Make a left on NW Saltzman Road. NW Saltzman Road ends at the gate at the trailhead, where it becomes a dirt and soft pine needle-strewn road.

RUN DESCRIPTION

This keyhole loop starts at the Lower Saltzman Gate. Proceed uphill on Saltzman Road (dirt). Go right on Maple Trail, then left on Quarry Trail to the Saltzman/Leif Erikson Drive junction. Continue straight (uphill)

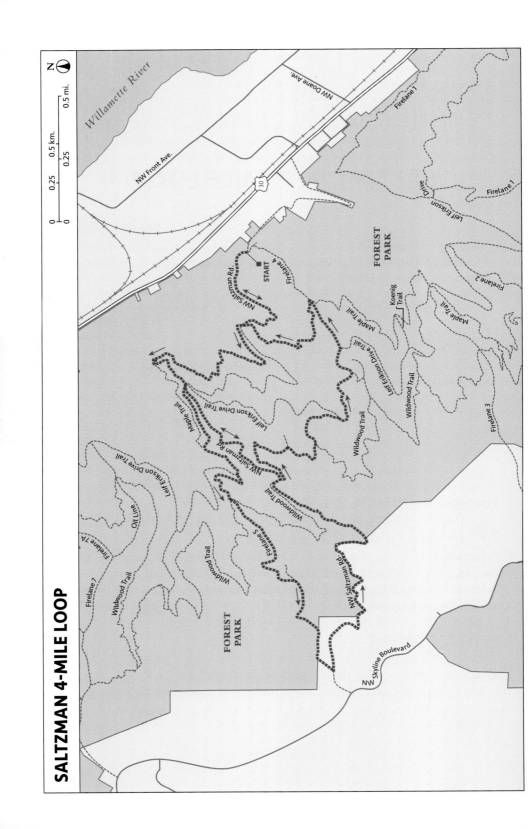

SALTZMAN 4-MILE LOOP

to Saltzman Road. Go left on Wildwood Trail; left on Cleater Trail; right on Leif Erikson Drive; left on Firelane 4; left on Maple Trail; and right on Saltzman Road, heading downhill to the gate. The first third is uphill, the middle third is flat, and the final third is downhill, providing a nice mix of elevation changes. The route is entirely in the forest and is a mix of single-track and fire road. There are no views.

LOWER SALTZMAN 10K LOOP

THE RUN DOWN

START: End of NW Saltzman Rd.; elevation 400 feet

OVERALL DISTANCE: 6.2-mile loop

APPROXIMATE RUNNING TIME: 1 hour

DIFFICULTY: Blue

ELEVATION GAIN: 883 feet

BEST SEASON TO RUN: Year-round

DOG FRIENDLY: Leashed dogs permitted

PARKING: Free

OTHER USERS: Cyclists

CELL PHONE COVERAGE: Good

MORE INFORMATION: www .forestparkconservancy.org

FINDING THE TRAILHEAD

If taking public transportation, take the #16 bus toward Sauvie Island and get off at the NW St. Helens and Saltzman stop. Run up NW Saltzman Road to the trailhead. You can also drive northwest out of Portland on NW St. Helens Road. Make a left on NW Saltzman Road. NW Saltzman Road ends at the gate at the trailhead, where it becomes a dirt and soft pine needle-strewn road.

RUN DESCRIPTION

This is a longer variation of the Saltzman 4-Mile Loop.

This keyhole loop starts at the Lower Saltzman Gate. Proceed uphill on Saltzman Road (dirt). Go right on Maple Trail and follow it to NW Firelane 5 Road, which switchbacks to Wildwood Trail, taking the leftmost of the three trails at the juncture. Stay on Wildwood, crossing NW Saltzman Road and then Cleater Trail, ignoring Firelane 4 on your left, until you come to Koenig Trail. Take Koenig Trail to the left, which leads over NW Leif Erikson Drive to a T with Maple Trail, where you head left (north) to complete the loop back to Saltzman Road and the start/finish point.

LOWER SALTZMAN 10K LOOP

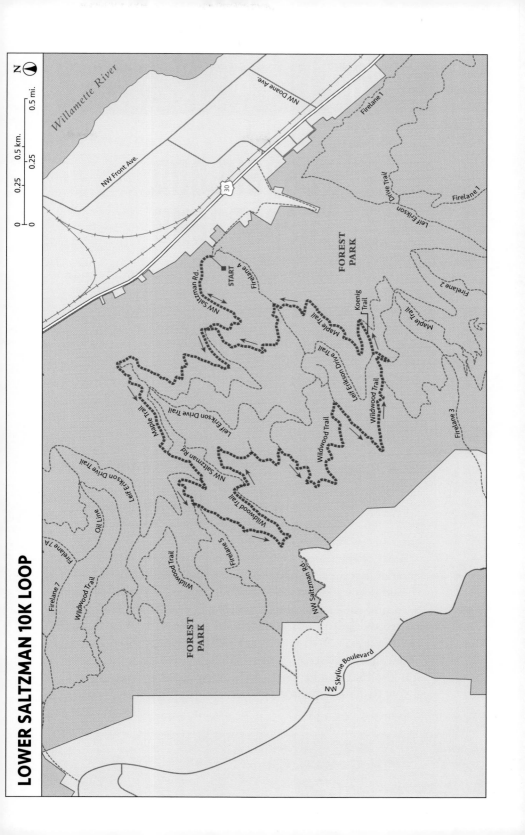

TerraiN aND TOPOGraPHY

The terrain of the areas we've covered in this guide are quite varied. That's one of the many beauties of the Portland metropolitan area and its different trail-running options: There are flat runs along waterfronts and mountain runs, and you can mix them to spice things up if you'd like. We've included quite a few of each, so you may select the perfect run to match your mood, or one with specific features if you are training for a specific event.

Portland area trails tend to be forested and prone to mud, although many have been rerouted to keep you from getting too wet or muddy. With some of the seasonal changes, Portland trail runners need to be adept at running on mud, runoff, rock, and occasional snow and ice. They must know how to confront water crossings and when to avoid dangerous ones. Similarly, they must be capable of maneuvering around roots, rocks, fallen branches; dealing with other trail obstacles; and handling wildlife confrontations.

Some of the trails in this guidebook are groomed and wide enough that they are practically dirt roads, while others are of the singletrack variety. Some allow dogs, others do not. Some turn into shoe-sucking mud when wet, others become rocky riverbeds. Still others attract local fauna during mating or nesting season. We request that you honor not only the notes about those trail sensitivities that we've provided in the guide, but also that you be very aware of the conditions and follow Leave No Trace practices in your trail running.

WILDWOOD AND LEIF 8.3-MILE FROM GERMANTOWN ROAD

THE RUN DOWN

START: Elevation 873 feet

OVERALL DISTANCE: 8.3-mile loop

APPROXIMATE RUNNING TIME: 1 hour, 20 minutes

DIFFICULTY: Blue

ELEVATION GAIN: 997 feet

BEST SEASON TO RUN: Year-round

DOG FRIENDLY: Leashed dogs permitted

PARKING: Free

OTHER USERS: Cyclists and equestrians on designated trails

CELL PHONE COVERAGE: Good

MORE INFORMATION: www .forestparkconservancy.org

PORTLAND

FINDING THE TRAILHEAD

From US 30, take NW Germantown Road north, through a couple tight turns, before finding parking on your left. The trailhead is readily accessible from the parking turnout.

RUN DESCRIPTION

This route follows a combination of buffed-out singletrack and good-quality dirt roads with a lot of pine-needle covering. You'll run through a heavily forested area, like most of Forest Park.

From the parking lot, run downhill on the Cannon Trail. Turn right on the butter-smooth, dirt NW Leif Erikson Drive. Turn right and run

WILDWOOD AND LEIF 8.3-MILE FROM GERMANTOWN ROAD

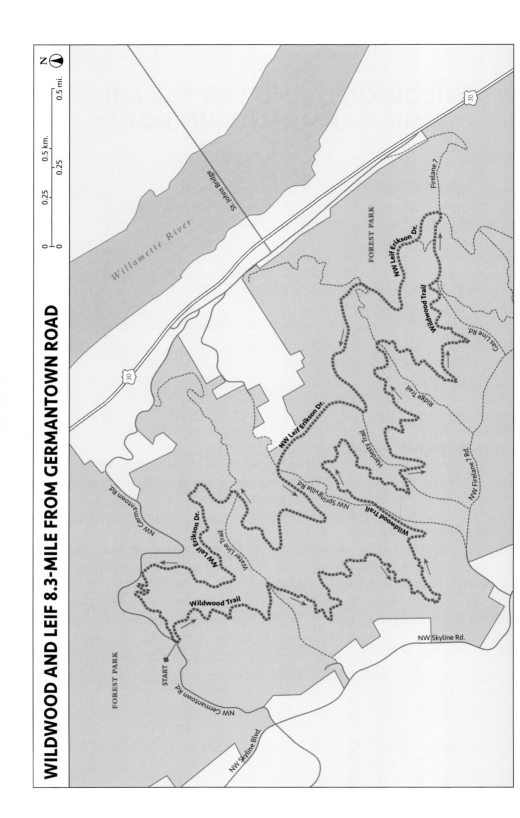

steeply uphill on the Gasline Trail. Turn right on the Wildwood Trail and follow it all the way back to the parking lot.

All trail junctions in Forest Park are clearly marked. NW Leif Erikson Drive even has white concrete posts with quarter-mile markers!

NORTH WILDWOOD 8.8-MILE

THE RUN DOWN

START: Wildwood trailhead; elevation 732 feet

OVERALL DISTANCE: 8.8-mile keyhole

APPROXIMATE RUNNING TIME: 90 minutes

DIFFICULTY: Blue

ELEVATION GAIN: 1,821 feet

BEST SEASON TO RUN: Year-round

DOG FRIENDLY: Leashed dogs permitted

PARKING: Free

OTHER USERS: Cyclists and equestrians on designated trails

CELL PHONE COVERAGE: Good

MORE INFORMATION: www .forestparkconservancy.org

FINDING THE TRAILHEAD

Head northwest from downtown Portland. Take NW St. Helens Road to Newberry Road, and follow Newberry Road to the Wildwood trailhead.

RUN DESCRIPTION

This part of Forest Park is bisected by a large power line. The clear-cut under the lines provides views to the north of the Willamette and Columbia Rivers, and to Mount Saint Helens and Mount Rainier. Some of the ascending is quite steep, as it heads directly uphill without switchbacks. The route is primarily on singletrack, with sections of primitive double-track (overgrown pathway). This is the least trafficked part of the Wildwood Trail; being farther from the city, this section provides a more primitive feel, with overgrown trees and vegetation that can wildly grow very close to the trail in the summer.

From the parking area, take the Wildwood Trail. Turn left on Firelane 15, right on Firelane 12, then left on the BPA Road. Follow the BPA Road

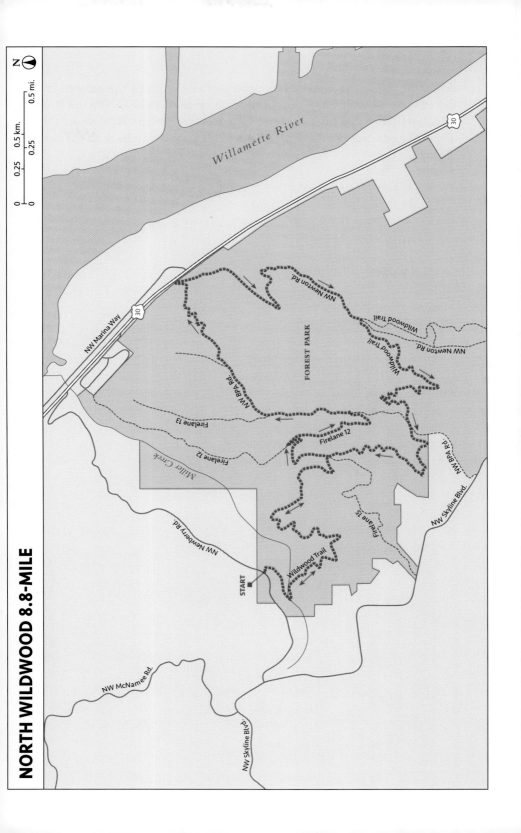

NORTH WILDWOOD 8.8-MILE

N

Willamette River

30

NW Marina Way

NW Newton Rd.

FOREST PARK

Wildwood Trail

Wildwood Trail

NW Newton Rd.

NW BPA Rd.

Firelane 13

Firelane 12

Firelane 12

NW BPA Rd.

NW Skyline Blvd.

Firelane 15

Miller Creek

NW Newberry Rd.

START

Wildwood Trail

NW McNamee Rd.

Nw Skyline Blvd.

0   0.25   0.5 km.

0   0.25   0.5 mi.

downhill, under the power lines, until you almost reach the heavily trafficked NW Saint Helens Road. Turn right on the dirt NW Newton Road,
which will take you back uphill to where you rejoin the Wildwood Trail.
Turn right on the Wildwood Trail and run all the way back to the parking area.

UPPER SALTZMAN 3-MILE

THE RUN DOWN

START: At the gate on NW Saltzman Rd.; elevation 1,125 feet

OVERALL DISTANCE: 3.0-mile loop

APPROXIMATE RUNNING TIME: 35 minutes

DIFFICULTY: Blue

ELEVATION GAIN: 459 feet

BEST SEASON TO RUN: Year-round

DOG FRIENDLY: Leashed dogs permitted

PARKING: Free

OTHER USERS: Cyclists and equestrians on designated trails

CELL PHONE COVERAGE: Good

MORE INFORMATION: www .forestparkconservancy.org

FINDING THE TRAILHEAD

Take NW Skyline Boulevard northwest from downtown Portland, and take a right on NW Saltzman Road. The parking lot is right at the gate. As the route name suggests, this follows the upper part of Saltzman Road.

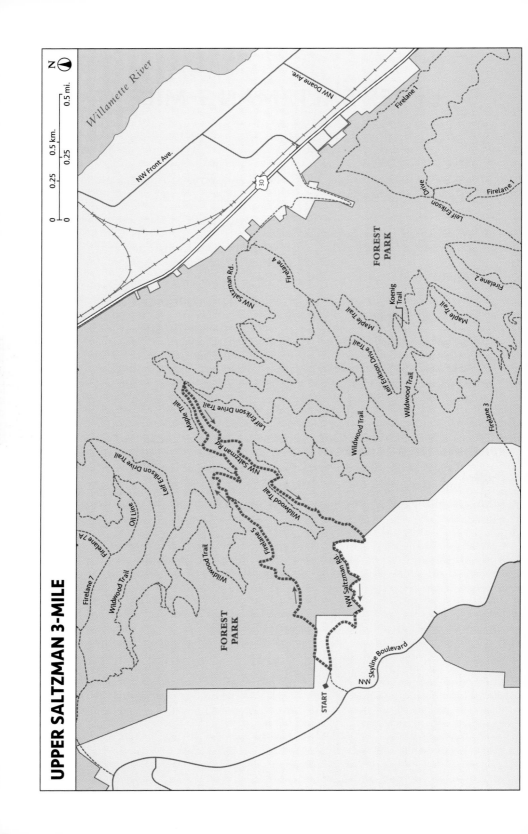

UPPER SALTZMAN 3-MILE

RUN DESCRIPTION

This run is mostly downhill to start and uphill to finish. Although this is a short run, the climbing and descending make it a bit more challenging. About 40 percent of the route is on singletrack and 60 percent on dirt road.

UPPER SALTZMAN 7.3-MILE

THE RUN DOWN

START: At the gate on NW Saltzman Rd.; elevation 1,096 feet

OVERALL DISTANCE: 7.3-mile loop

APPROXIMATE RUNNING TIME: 75 minutes

DIFFICULTY: Blue

ELEVATION GAIN: 1,161 feet

BEST SEASON TO RUN: Year-round

DOG FRIENDLY: Leashed dogs permitted

PARKING: Free

OTHER USERS: Cyclists and equestrians on designated trails

CELL PHONE COVERAGE: Good

MORE INFORMATION: www .forestparkconservancy.org

FINDING THE TRAILHEAD

Take NW Skyline Boulevard northwest from downtown Portland and take a right on NW Saltzman Road. The parking lot is right at the gate; no restrooms, services, or water are available. As the name suggests, this is the upper part of Saltzman Road.

RUN DESCRIPTION

This route is similar to the Upper Saltzman 3-Mile, but is a bit longer. One of the least busy trailheads into Forest Park, Upper Saltzman is a great starting point for runners who want an easy (i.e., all downhill) start to their runs. Heavily forested, the trails leading from Upper Saltzman are cool and shaded on hot summer days.

Run downhill on Firelane 5; turn left on the Wildwood Trail; turn right on Firelane 7; and continue straight on the NW Oil Line Road until it meets NW Leif Erikson Drive. Turn right on NW Leif Erickson Drive; turn right on NW Saltzman Road, and run uphill to the parking area.

UPPER SALTZMAN 7.3-MILE LOOP

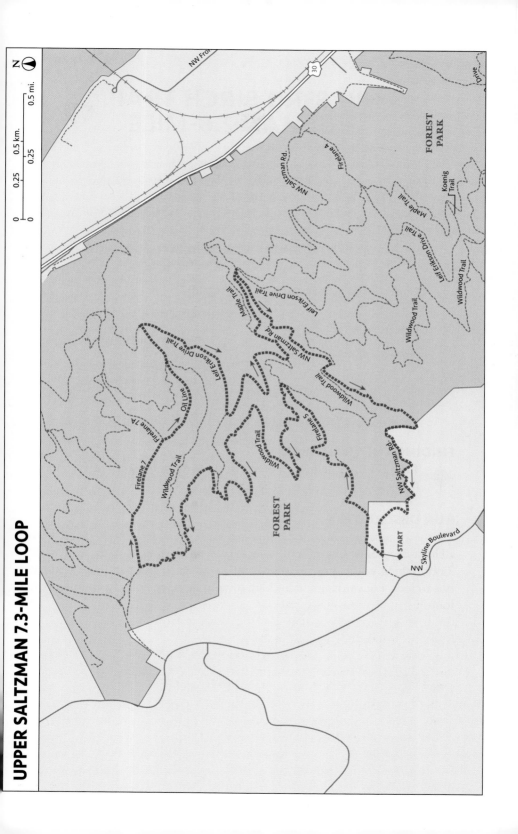

NW 53RD BIRCH TRAIL HOLMAN 2.6-MILE

THE RUN DOWN

START: Trailhead on NW 53rd Dr.; elevation 840 feet

OVERALL DISTANCE: 2.6-mile loop

APPROXIMATE RUNNING TIME: 40 minutes

DIFFICULTY: Blue

ELEVATION GAIN: 551 feet

BEST SEASON TO RUN: Year-round

DOG FRIENDLY: Leashed dogs permitted

PARKING: Free

OTHER USERS: Cyclists

CELL PHONE COVERAGE: Good

MORE INFORMATION: www
.forestparkconservancy.org

FINDING THE TRAILHEAD

 Take NW Cornell Road out of downtown Portland. Turn right on NW 53rd Drive to reach the trailhead.

RUN DESCRIPTION

This is a short loop ideal for hill climb workouts up Holman. Begin with a short drop onto Birch Trail, then take your first right onto Wildwood Trail, which will curve clockwise until you reach Holman Lane at about one o'clock. Follow Holman back up to your starting point to complete the loop.

NW 53RD BIRCH TRAIL HOLMAN 2.6-MILE

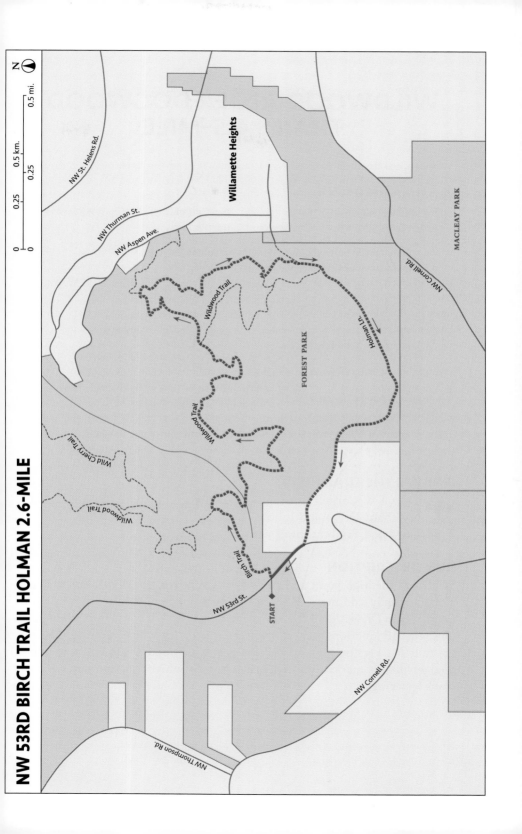

WILDWOOD ALDER DOGWOOD TRAILS 4.5-MILE

THE RUN DOWN

START: Wild Cherry Trail/ Dogwood trailhead; elevation 909 feet

OVERALL DISTANCE: 4.5 miles round trip

APPROXIMATE RUNNING TIME: 45 minutes

DIFFICULTY: Green

ELEVATION GAIN: 468 feet

BEST SEASON TO RUN: Year-round

DOG FRIENDLY: Leashed dogs permitted

PARKING: Free

OTHER USERS: Mountain bikers and equestrians on designated trails

CELL PHONE COVERAGE: Good

MORE INFORMATION: www .portlandoregon.gov/parks/ finder/index.cfm?action=View Park&PropertyID=127

FINDING THE TRAILHEAD

Take NW Cornell Road out of downtown Portland. Turn right on NW 53rd Drive and follow NW 53rd Drive to the Wild Cherry Trail/Dogwood Trail trailhead signs.

RUN DESCRIPTION

Start near the high point and run down, up, down, up, all on singletrack. You can easily add more distance by continuing on Wildwood Trail or Leif Erikson Drive. All of the signage in Forest Park is consistent throughout, with all junctions marked by green signs with white lettering. There are mile markers on the Leif Erikson and Wildwood Trails. (In fact, each quarter-mile is marked on Leif Erikson with white concrete posts with black lettering.)

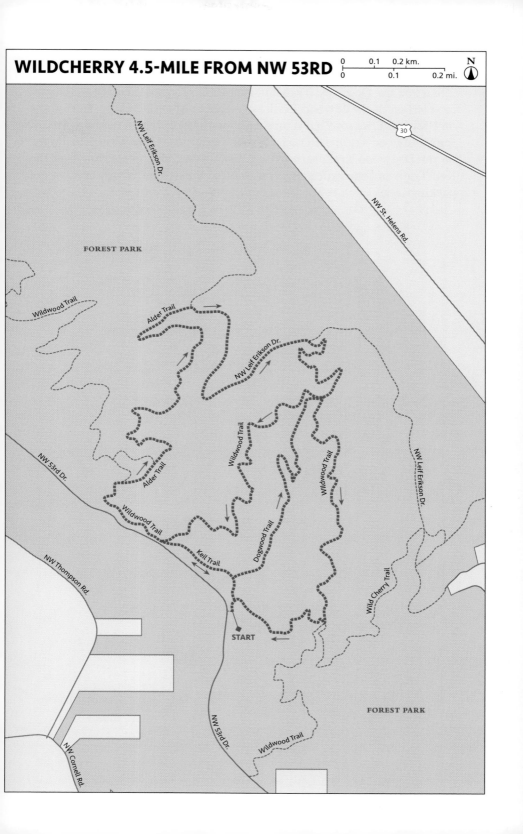

Start on the Dogwood Trail and run uphill. Turn left on the Keil Trail; turn left on the Wildwood Trail; turn right on the Alder Trail. Turn right on NW Leif Erickson Drive; turn right on the Dogwood Trail; turn left on the Wildwood Trail; then turn right on the Wild Cherry Trail. Turn right on the Dogwood Trail; turn left on the Wildwood Trail; turn left on the Keil Trail; and then turn right on the Dogwood Trail to run back to the parking area.

KINGS HEIGHTS CITY TRAIL

THE RUN DOWN

START: Barista Coffee Shop; elevation 151 feet

OVERALL DISTANCE: 4.5-mile loop

APPROXIMATE RUNNING TIME: 60 minutes

DIFFICULTY: Blue

ELEVATION GAIN: 889 feet

BEST SEASON TO RUN: Year-round

DOG FRIENDLY: Leashed dogs permitted

PARKING: Free

OTHER USERS: Hikers, cyclists, and cars on road sections; no bikes allowed on trails

CELL PHONE COVERAGE: Good

MORE INFORMATION: http://pittockmansion.org

FINDING THE TRAILHEAD

 Start from the Barista Coffee Shop at 823 NW 23rd Ave. in Northwest Portland.

RUN DESCRIPTION

Run stairs and trails to the historic Pittock Mansion. The route through the neighborhood (Kings Heights) is paved. All of the trails within Macleay Park are dirt and singletrack in heavily forested terrain. The footing is easy, but there is a lot of vertical. There are three staircases to ascend along the route. Overall the route is 60 percent road and 40 percent trail.

From the finish at Pittock Mansion, you can enjoy magnificent views—in fact, the best in the city—on a clear day. Mount Rainier and Mount Saint Helens are to the north, downtown Portland and Mount Hood are to the east. This area has one of the highest densities of restaurants, coffee shops, breweries, bars, and boutiques in the city. People venture here from all over the region to enjoy these amenities.

From Barista Coffee Shop, go west on NW Kearney Street, then right on NW 24th Avenue. Go left on NW Marshall Street, then left on NW 26th Avenue, and then up the staircase at the end of NW 26th. Go right on NW

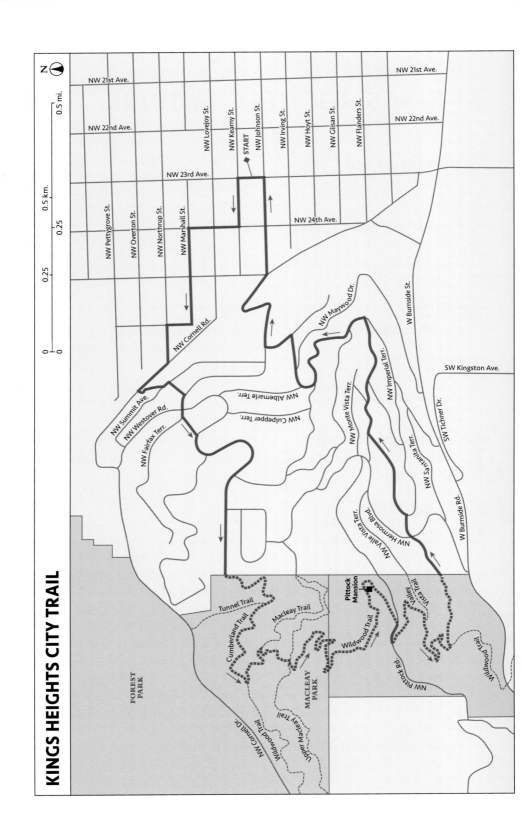

KINGS HEIGHTS CITY TRAIL

Cornell Road, left on NW Summit Court, and then left on NW Summit Avenue. Look for steep staircase on the right, go up the stairs, and then go right on NW Westover Road.

Go straight at the four-way intersection and continue on NW Fairfax Terrace. Look for the stairs to the left just after the junction, and ascend the stairs to take a right on NW Cumberland Road. NW Cumberland Road ends where Cumberland Trail begins. Follow Cumberland Trail, turning left on Wildwood Trail. Follow Wildwood Trail to Pittock Mansion at the summit.

To return, continue on Wildwood Trail toward the Oregon Zoo. Turn left on Verde Vista (a dirt road that becomes paved). Turn right on NW Beuhla Vista Terrace; left on NW Macleay Boulevard; right on NW Albemarle Terrace; right on NW Melinda Avenue; right on NW Westover Road; left on NW Johnson Street, and finally, left on NW 23rd Avenue.

WaTer CrossinGs

Do you recall running through large puddles—or even small ponds—as a child? If so, then perhaps you mastered the technique of taking exaggerated steps with a cartoonlike form that kept you relatively dry while making everyone near you wet. That skill is invaluable, and if you don't have it down, take advantage of the dampness that Portland offers and hone it. Go to a shallow stream, puddle, or other body of water that is not more than 6 inches deep. Think of lizards that nature programs always show running in slow motion across water. Try to duplicate that high-stepping form, and throw a little lateral kick at the end of each stride to push the water away.

For deeper water crossings, decide whether it is worth trying to stay dry. The water and air temperature, the width of the body of water, the rate of the current or flow, the availability of an alternative crossing, and the amount of time you can afford should factor into your decision. Also remember that going around water crossings, puddles, or wet areas causes erosion.

If you don't want to take the time to keep your feet dry or to change socks, consider the "easy in/easy out" alternative. Wearing highly breathable footwear or trail-running shoes with mesh uppers allows water to penetrate the shoe when confronting water crossings but also allows water to exit quickly. Water will be effectively squeegeed out of the shoe by running on dry terrain, and after a mile or two the recent drenching will be only a faint memory. Wearing wool socks, especially ones made with merino wool that does not itch, will maintain a moderate temperature for your feet regardless of whether they are wet or dry. They will also help prevent blisters because of their temperature-regulating attributes.

BEYOND PORTLAND

WASHINGTON

The scenic Columbia River separates Portland, Oregon, from communities in southern Washington, including Vancouver and Camas. The Washington runs included in this guide are easily reached from Portland, and explore the north side of the Columbia River Gorge as well as other open spaces and parks that provide excellent trail running opportunities.

SILVER STAR MOUNTAIN 4-MILE

THE RUN DOWN

START: NF-4019 Silver Star Trailhead; elevation 3,494 feet

OVERALL DISTANCE: 3.8-mile keyhole

APPROXIMATE RUNNING TIME: 50 minutes

DIFFICULTY: Blue

ELEVATION GAIN: 938 feet

BEST SEASON TO RUN: Spring, summer, fall

DOG FRIENDLY: Leashed dogs permitted

PARKING: Free

OTHER USERS: Mountain biking on designated trails at the ski area

CELL PHONE COVERAGE: Poor

MORE INFORMATION: www .wta.org/go-hiking/hikes/ silver-star-mountain#trail head-map

FINDING THE TRAILHEAD

Although this is a difficult area to navigate, if putting Silver Star Trailhead into Google Maps, it is easily located (NF-4019 Silver Star Trailhead). Warning: Access is via a rough road; a high-clearance vehicle is required. There are two trailheads at this location; Grouse Mountain is the other.

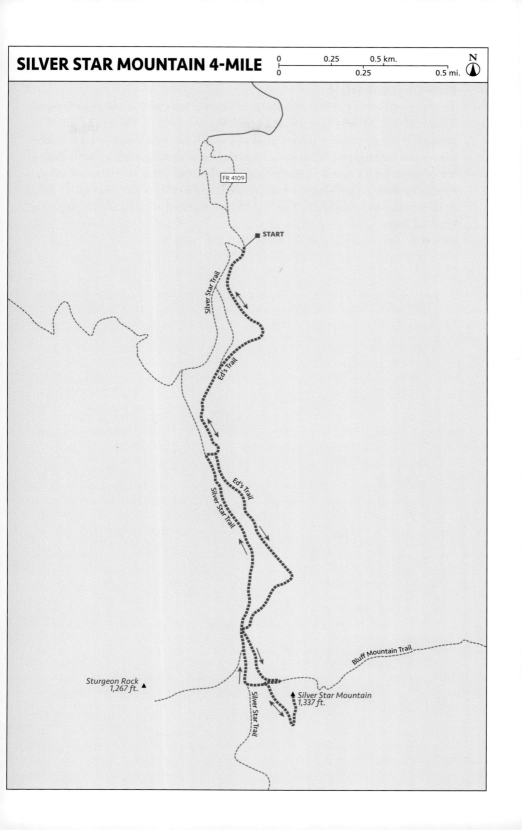

SILVER STAR MOUNTAIN 4-MILE

0   0.25   0.5 km.
0   0.25   0.5 mi.

N

FR 4109

START

Silver Star Trail

Ed's Trail

Ed's Trail

Silver Star Trail

Bluff Mountain Trail

Sturgeon Rock ▲
1,267 ft.

Silver Star Trail

▲ Silver Star Mountain
1,337 ft.

RUN DESCRIPTION

This route features amazing geological formations and stunning views of Mount Hood, Mount Saint Helens, and Mount Adams. The trail, which is primarily singletrack, is pretty rocky, though not much in the trees so the views can be enjoyed. There is a smattering of doubletrack as well. Not a lot of switchbacks; this is rather a gradual climb. This is truly a must-do venue. In mid- to late June, a special event (similar to a Fat Ass run) is held at this area on the solstice. The wildflowers are in abundance during this time of year.

HERITAGE TRAIL AT LACAMAS LAKE

An out-and-back run on the relatively flat 3.5-mile Heritage Trail is the perfect segue to advance to the more challenging 6 miles of terrain in the Round Lake system in Lacamas Lake Regional Park. Whereas the Heritage Trail is on the west side of Lacamas Lake, which is north of NE Everett Street, Round Lake is on the south side of NE Everett Street. In addition to wide rolling paths, there are singletrack trails through the forest and through open meadows with blooming lilies in the springtime.

THE RUN DOWN

START: Heritage trailhead adjacent to Lacamas Lake; elevation 194 feet

OVERALL DISTANCE: 3.0 miles out and back

APPROXIMATE RUNNING TIME: 30 minutes

DIFFICULTY: Green

ELEVATION GAIN: 93 feet

BEST SEASON TO RUN: Year-round

DOG FRIENDLY: Leashed dogs permitted

PARKING: Free

OTHER USERS: No equestrians; mountain bikes allowed

CELL PHONE COVERAGE: Very good

MORE INFORMATION: www .clark.wa.gov/public-works/ lacamas-lake-regional- park#expand

FINDING THE TRAILHEAD

Park at the lot on NE Lake Road in Camas. Follow the pathway to the Heritage Trail on the west side of the lake. It is a short walk from the parking lot.

HERITAGE TRAIL AT LACAMAS LAKE

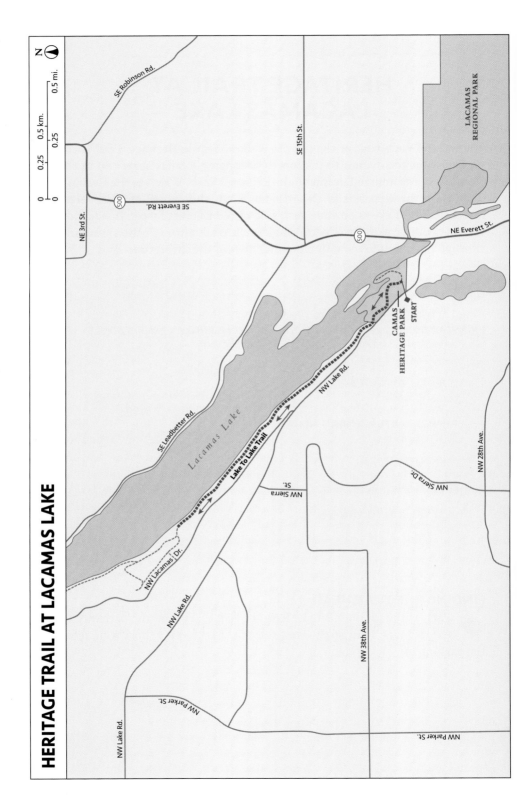

RUN DESCRIPTION

This trail is hard-packed gravel for the majority of the distance and flanks Lacamas Lake on the west side. It is not completely flat, and there are some sections of exposed tree roots. As an out-and-back run, it is a great trail for beginners. The Clark County Running Club (http://clarkcountyrunning club.org/) hosts events on this route, as well as on the Round Lake trails.

ROUND LAKE TRAIL

THE RUN DOWN

START: Adjacent to the parking lot at 3344 NE Everett St. in Camas; elevation 188 feet

OVERALL DISTANCE: 5.2 miles in multiple loops

APPROXIMATE RUNNING TIME: 60 minutes

DIFFICULTY: Green

ELEVATION GAIN: 787 feet

BEST SEASON TO RUN: Year-round

DOG FRIENDLY: Leashed dogs permitted

PARKING: Free

OTHER USERS: Equestrians and mountain bikers. Trails for foot traffic only are marked.

CELL PHONE COVERAGE: Good

MORE INFORMATION: www .alltrails.com/trail/us/ washington/lacamas-lake-and -round-lake

FINDING THE TRAILHEAD

Located at 3344 NE Everett Street in Camas, Washington, the trailhead is located adjacent to the parking lot, which provides spaces for twenty-five cars. There is additional free parking across the street near the Heritage Trail or just north over the bridge on NE Everett Street behind the market.

RUN DESCRIPTION

Round Lake trails cover a variety of terrain, weaving in and out of the forest and through wide, open meadows. Even though 80 percent of the singletrack trails are unmarked, they are worthy of exploration. Springtime is an ideal time to run this route, with a variety of blooming flowers, highlighted by a gorgeous field of camas lilies. During the rainy season, some of the singletrack trails can get rather muddy and slick in spots.

Begin on the wide pathway near the playground, head south over the bridge at the dam, and continue along the southern lip of Round Lake. Follow the lake to Lake Trail, which has many spines and fingers, keeping in mind that there are options to take more technical singletrack or to stick

ROUND LAKE TRAIL

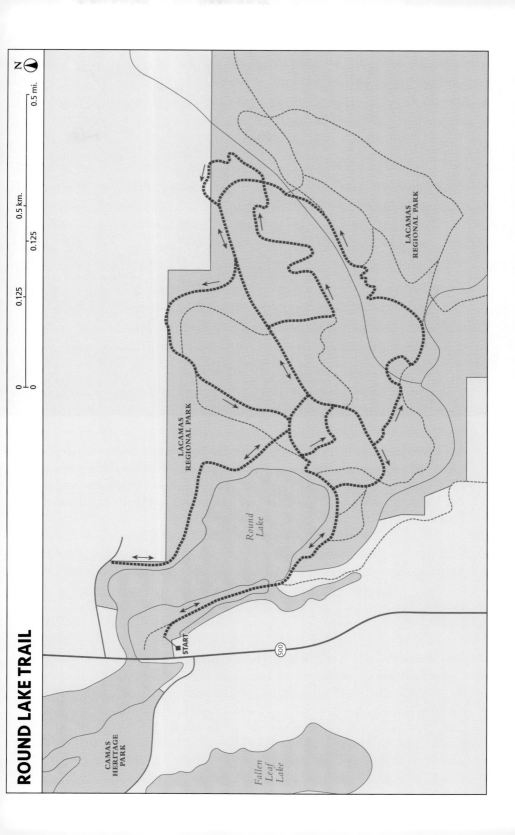

to the wider pathways closer to the lake. Complete a short loop around Round Lake, or wander to the trails farther south, which include the camas lily fields, as well as Woodburn Falls and the Lower Falls. Spend an hour or longer crisscrossing the various trail segments to experience the entire park.

PACKS, HYDRATION SYSTEMS, GEL FLASKS, AND WATER FILTERS

Given the paucity of water fountains, spigots, or other conveniences on the typical trail run, most trail runners who run long enough to build up a thirst or hunger carry liquid and nutritional reserves. Depending on the temperature, projected length of run, availability of potable water, and the particular hydration and nutritional needs of an individual trail runner, it may be necessary to carry substantial quantities of drink and food on an excursion.

For shorter outings, a trail runner is likely to be able to get by without any liquids or food. But as temperatures rise and the distance of a run lengthens, trail runners will, at a minimum, need to carry a 16- or 20-ounce bottle or flask of water or electrolyte-replacement sports drink. Depending on preference, bottles may be carried in hand, either by simply gripping the bottle or with the assistance of a strap that fastens the bottle around the back of the hand, or in a lumbar or "fanny" pack. Modern lumbar packs are designed to distribute weight evenly throughout the lumbar region and often feature straight or angled pouches for bottles and separate pockets for food, clothing, and accessories. Some lumbar packs also include "gel holsters" for runners who carry a gel flask. Gel flasks hold up to five packs of sports gel for easy consumption and offer relief from sticky fingers or the need to pack out trash.

For longer runs, especially on trails that do not come in contact with sources of potable water, a hydration pack or multibottle carrier is probably necessary. Hydration packs have become common accessories in the evolving world of endurance sports because of their convenience and functionality. They incorporate a bladder or reservoir, delivery tube or hose, and a bite valve that allow trail runners to carry substantial quantities of fluid that are evenly distributed and consumed with hands-free ease. Other systems use a number of soft flasks that shrink when their contents are consumed. These packs are built more as form-fitting vests, with the flasks carried on the chest for easy access.

Hydration packs range in size and carrying capacity and come as backpacks, lumbar packs, and sports vests. Many hydration packs offer additional volume and storage pouches for food, clothing, and other trail necessities or conveniences. Certain bite valves are easier to use than others, and some bladders are difficult to clean or keep free of bacteria, mold, mildew, and fungus. Others come with antimicrobial compounds, and some feature in-line water filters.

When running on trails that cross water sources, whether streams, creeks, rivers, ponds, lakes, or merely large puddles, trail runners can free themselves of substantial weight by carrying water filters and a single water bottle. Make sure the filter removes such evils as cryptosporidium, giardia, E. coli, volatile organic compounds, and other threatening substances common to the area where it is likely to be used. Note, however, that water filters do not protect against viruses. It may be necessary to use a combination of iodine tablets with a filter to assure the water is safe for consumption. Other devices use a charge to purify the water; another alternative is to use a filtered straw that allows you to pull filtered water directly from the source.

CAPE HORN/NANCY RUSSELL OVERLOOK 4.8-MILE

THE RUN DOWN

START: Skamania County Public Transit and Ride; elevation 541 feet

OVERALL DISTANCE: 4.8 miles out and back

APPROXIMATE RUNNING TIME: 45 to 60 minutes

DIFFICULTY: Blue

ELEVATION GAIN: 1,063 feet

BEST SEASON TO RUN: Late summer, fall, early winter; sections of the route are closed February to July for falcon season

DOG FRIENDLY: Leashed dogs permitted

PARKING: Free

OTHER USERS: None

CELL COVERAGE: Poor

MORE INFORMATION: www.wta.org/go-hiking/hikes/cape-horn

FINDING THE TRAILHEAD

Parking is at the Skamania County Public Transit and Ride, at the intersection of Salmon Falls Road and WA 14. From downtown Portland, take either WA 14E, or I-84 and WA 14E, for a drive of about forty minutes. Take a left on Salmon Falls Road, and parking is to your immediate right.

RUN DESCRIPTION

From the trailhead off Salmon Falls Road, this out-and-back run starts with an almost thousand-foot ascent, complete with switchbacks, to afford stunning views of Hamilton Mountain, Beacon Rock, and the Columbia River Gorge. The Cape Horn Trail is easy to follow and, once you get past

CAPE HORN/NANCY RUSSELL OVERLOOK 4.8-MILE

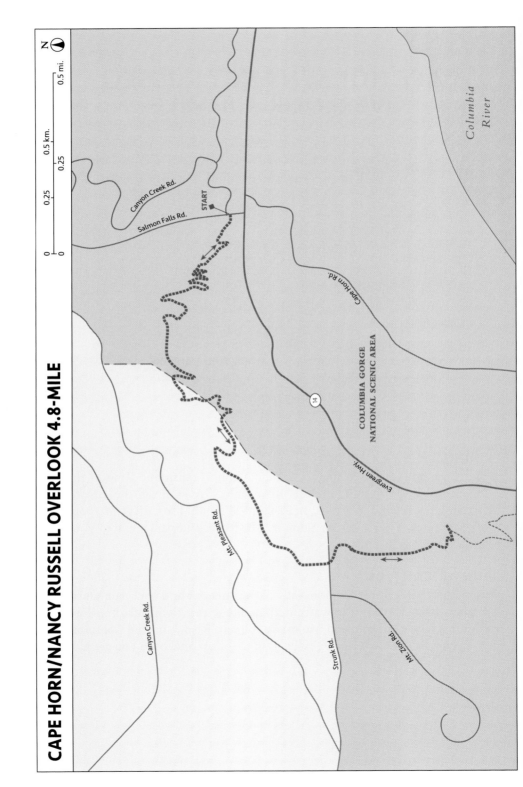

the first mile-and-a-half of climbing, very runnable. The two middle miles include an overlook platform that honors the founder of the Friends of the Gorge, Nancy Russell, who headed up a twenty-year campaign to preserve the land for public access. The land is habitat for peregrine falcons and Larch Mountain salamanders.

NANCY'S 5.4-MILE OUT-AND-BACK AT LUCIA FALLS

Located in Yacolt, Washington, 387-acre Moulton Falls Regional Park sits at the confluence of the East Fork of the Lewis River and Big Tree Creek and provides a relatively flat out-and-back pathway from the parking lot off Lucia Falls Road. The parking only accommodates eleven cars, so you need to arrive early to secure a spot or go to the Hantwick Road parking lot, where there are more parking spots. It is common to see eagles perched on tree branches seeking their next meal of fish, which they can track in the adjacent waterway. If visiting this area on weekends, stop at Pomeroy Cellars for a wine tasting.

THE RUN DOWN

START: 27781 NE Lucia Falls Rd. in Yacolt; elevation 542 feet

OVERALL DISTANCE: 5.4 miles out and back

APPROXIMATE RUNNING TIME: 60 minutes

DIFFICULTY: Green

ELEVATION GAIN: 210 feet

BEST SEASON TO RUN: Year-round

DOG FRIENDLY: Leashed dogs permitted

PARKING: Free parking in eleven spots, with a short walk to the trailhead

OTHER USERS: Equestrians, mountain bikers

CELL PHONE COVERAGE: Good

MORE INFORMATION: www .clark.wa.gov/public-works/ moulton-falls-regional-park

FINDING THE TRAILHEAD

Park in the lot located at 27781 NE Lucia Falls Road in Yacolt. Signage at the parking area directs you to nearby restrooms and trails. The trailhead is located just across a walking bridge through the forest.

NANCY'S 5.4-MILE OUT-AND-BACK AT LUCIA FALLS

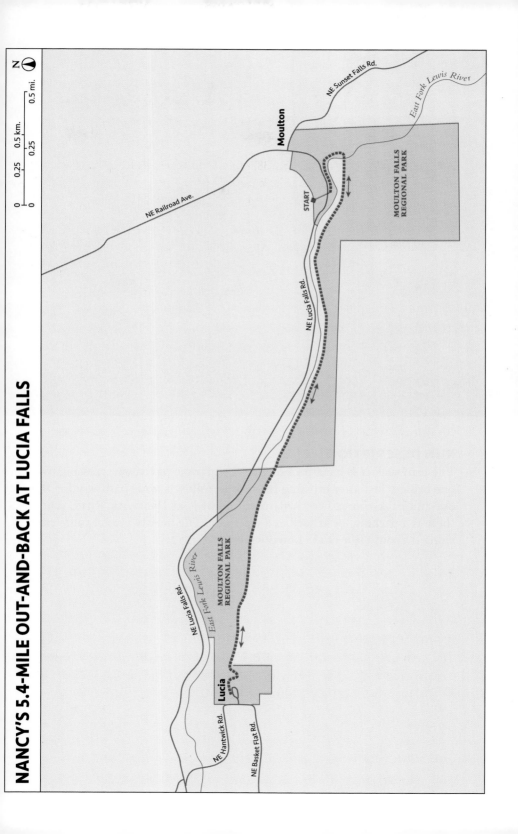

RUN DESCRIPTION

The trail surface is hard-packed gravel and some pavement, crossing over one bridge. Just after crossing the bridge, follow a wide pathway for this out-and-back route. The turnaround point is at Hantwick Road, where there is a parking lot as well as a restroom. The mostly gravel route runs along the south side of the Lewis River.

BELLS MOUNTAIN OUT-AND-BACK

The 7.5-mile Bells Mountain Trail can be accessed from Lucia Falls to the north or from Rock Creek Park to the south, where it connects to the 24.7-mile Tarbell Trail. Follow singletrack trails through fir and alder forest, over short bridges, and through open meadows with views of Mount Saint Helens and Mount Adams on a clear day. The trail is marked every half-mile and is very well maintained.

THE RUN DOWN

START: Trailhead at Lucia Falls; elevation 531 feet

OVERALL DISTANCE: 4.1 miles out and back

APPROXIMATE RUNNING TIME: 45 minutes

DIFFICULTY: Blue

ELEVATION GAIN: 1,242 feet

BEST SEASON TO RUN: Year-round; some muddy and slick spots during heavy rains

DOG FRIENDLY: Leashed dogs permitted

PARKING: Free in the small parking lot

OTHER USERS: Equestrians, mountain bikers

CELL PHONE COVERAGE: Good

MORE INFORMATION: www .clark.wa.gov/sites/all/files/ public-works/Parks/moulton_ bellsmttarbell.pdf

FINDING THE TRAILHEAD

Access for this trail is at Lucia Falls. Park in the lot located at 27781 NE Lucia Falls Road in Yacolt. Signage at the parking area directs you to nearby restrooms and trails. The trailhead is located just across a walking bridge through the forest. Cross the walking bridge and follow the gravel pathway to a well-marked turnoff for the Bells Mountain Trail, heading away from the Lewis River on an uphill route.

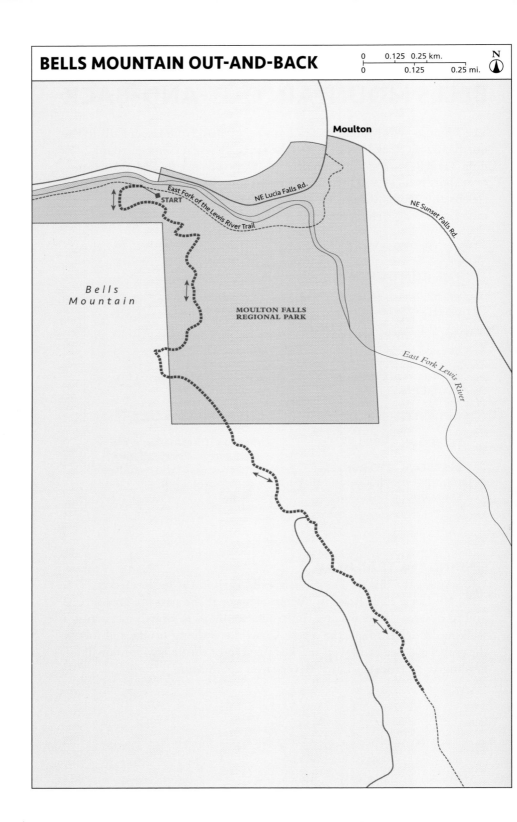

BELLS MOUNTAIN OUT-AND-BACK

Moulton

East Fork of the Lewis River Trail

NE Lucia Falls Rd.

NE Sunset Falls Rd.

START

Bells
Mountain

MOULTON FALLS
REGIONAL PARK

East Fork Lewis River

RUN DESCRIPTION

This glorious singletrack trail features winding and sweeping switchbacks marked at every half-mile interval. Cross several footbridges, and enjoy the lush forest of fir and alder before reaching an open area providing glimpses of Mount Saint Helens and Mount Adams on a clear day. The elevation gain—boasting more than a 20-percent grade in spots—is well worth the effort, as you will experience amazing panoramic vistas from the higher segments of this trail. This route is an out-and-back run, but, if you choose, you can extend it by continuing to the Tarbell Trail for additional mileage up to a 24.7-mile loop. There are also junctures on the route for additional viewpoints or more mileage.

HAMILTON MOUNTAIN 6.7-MILE

THE RUN DOWN

START: At the trailhead next to the parking lot; elevation 505 feet

OVERALL DISTANCE: 6.7-mile keyhole

APPROXIMATE RUNNING TIME: 100 minutes

DIFFICULTY: Blue

ELEVATION GAIN: 2,083 feet

BEST SEASON TO RUN: Spring, summer, fall

DOG FRIENDLY: Leashed dogs permitted (off-leash pets are ticketed)

PARKING: A fee is charged

OTHER USERS: None

CELL PHONE COVERAGE: Poor

MORE INFORMATION: http://parks.state.wa.us/474/Beacon-Rock

FINDING THE TRAILHEAD

Traveling on WA 14, continue uphill from the Beacon Rock State Park entrance sign for 0.5 mile, and park in the lot on the right. The trailhead is next to the parking lot. There are restroom facilities.

RUN DESCRIPTION

This run features a gradual to steep ascent to the Pool of the Winds (a waterfall area) on a singletrack trail. Along the way there are several different route options, all marked with signs. Continue climbing, approaching some rocky outcroppings, and then continue to the exposed summit of Hamilton Mountain. On a clear day enjoy views of Mount Hood. Wildflowers are in abundance in the springtime. Enjoy a fun, downhill singletrack trail weaving through the woods on the Dawn's Cutoff Trail. Except for the summit, the majority of the route is within the trees.

HAMILTON MOUNTAIN 6.7-MILE

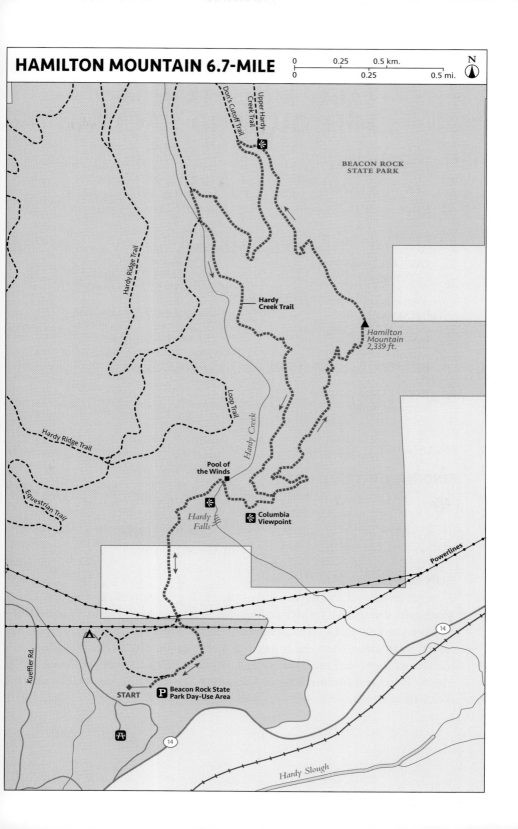

BEACON ROCK
STATE PARK

Don's Cutoff Trail

Upper Hardy
Creek Trail

Hardy Ridge Trail

Hardy
Creek Trail

Hamilton
Mountain
2,339 ft.

Loop Trail

Hardy Ridge Trail

Hardy Creek

Equestrian Trail

Pool of
the Winds

Hardy
Falls

Columbia
Viewpoint

Powerlines

Kueffler Rd.

14

START

P Beacon Rock State
Park Day-Use Area

14

Hardy Slough

TABLE MOUNTAIN 14-MILE OUT-AND-BACK

THE RUN DOWN

START: Near the Bridge of the Gods parking area; elevation 128 feet

OVERALL DISTANCE: 14 miles out and back

APPROXIMATE RUNNING TIME: 3 to 4 hours

DIFFICULTY: Blue

ELEVATION GAIN: 3,944 feet

BEST SEASON TO RUN: Spring, summer, fall

DOG FRIENDLY: Leashed dogs permitted

PARKING: Free

OTHER USERS: No mountain bikers; equestrians permitted

CELL PHONE COVERAGE: Poor

MORE INFORMATION: www .wta.org/go-hiking/hikes/ table-mountain-3

FINDING THE TRAILHEAD

There are a few different access points for this route. Free parking is available near the intersection of WA 14 and the Pacific Crest Trail (PCT), on the Washington side of the Columbia River just across the Bridge of the Gods. The trailhead is located near this point.

RUN DESCRIPTION

This route follows singletrack along the PCT, gradually ascending Table Mountain. Run through thick ferns, cross over streams on footbridges, and continue ascending to an exposed final rocky ascent of Table Mountain. Enjoy great views from the top of this iconic mountain on the Washington side of the Columbia River Gorge. When it is clear, there are views of Mount Hood and Mount Adams. This route is within the forest until the rocky final ascent.

TABLE MOUNTAIN 14-MILE OUT-AND-BACK

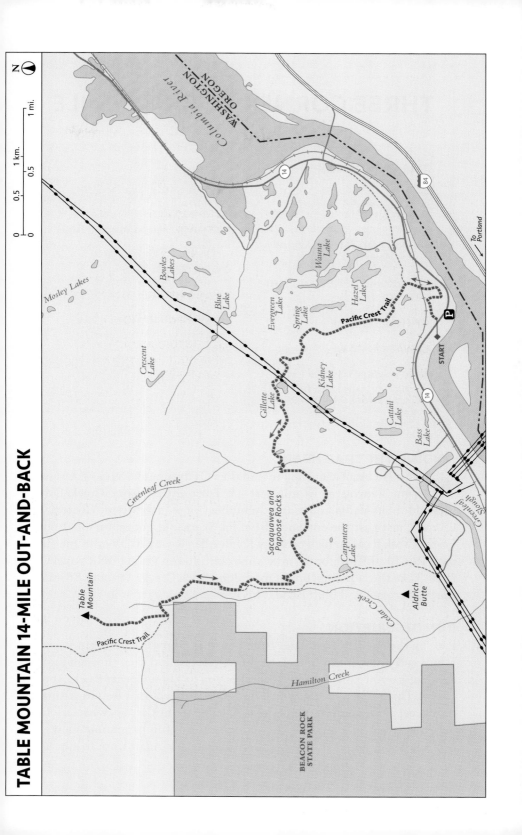

Table Mountain

Pacific Crest Trail

Mosley Lakes

Boules Lakes

Crescent Lake

Blue Lake

Gillette Lake

Greenleaf Creek

Sacaquawea and Papoose Rocks

Evergreen Lake

Spring Lake

Kidney Lake

Carpenters Lake

Hamilton Creek

Cedar Creek

Aldrich Butte

BEACON ROCK STATE PARK

Wauna Lake

Hazel Lake

Pacific Crest Trail

Cattail Lake

Bass Lake

Greenleaf Slough

START

Columbia River

WASHINGTON
OREGON

14

84

To Portland

N

0   0.5   1 km.
0   0.5   1 mi.

THREE CORNER ROCK 8.7-MILE

THE RUN DOWN

START: Pacific Crest Tr. crossing on Red Bluff Rd.; elevation 1,450 feet

OVERALL DISTANCE: 8.7 miles out and back

APPROXIMATE RUNNING TIME: 75 to 100 minutes

DIFFICULTY: Black

ELEVATION GAIN: 2,195 feet

BEST SEASON TO RUN: Late spring, summer, and fall

DOG FRIENDLY: Leashed dogs permitted

PARKING: Free parking on Red Bluff Rd.

OTHER USERS: None

CELL COVERAGE: Poor

MORE INFORMATION: www .wta.org/go-hiking/hikes/ cape-horn

FINDING THE TRAILHEAD

This is a bit of a journey to find the PCT trailhead. Drive WA 14 east from Vancouver to milepost 43. Turn left on Rock Creek Drive (signed for Skamania Lodge and Columbia Gorge Interpretive Center). At 0.3 mile, just past the entrance drive for Skamania Lodge, turn left onto Foster Creek Road (which becomes Ryan Allen Road). At 0.9 mile, turn left onto Red Bluff Road for 0.3 mile, then continue on gravel DNR Road CG 2000. Take this winding, uphill road along Rock Creek. At about 8.5 miles, the PCT crosses Red Bluff Road. This is where you start your run.

RUN DESCRIPTION

Pick up the Pacific Coast Trail from a former clear-cut and begin what is just over 4 miles of climbing, first through forest and then through drainages, before you gain the ridge that takes you to Three Corner Rock. At the base of Three Corner Rock, you'll find concrete steps that lead to within a dozen feet of the summit. You can easily climb to the flat top, where a lookout tower was once affixed. The summit affords full panoramic views of Mounts Hood, Jefferson, Rainier, Saint Helens, and Adams, not to mention

THREE CORNER ROCK 8.7-MILE

0   0.25   0.5 km.
0   0.25   0.5 mi.

N

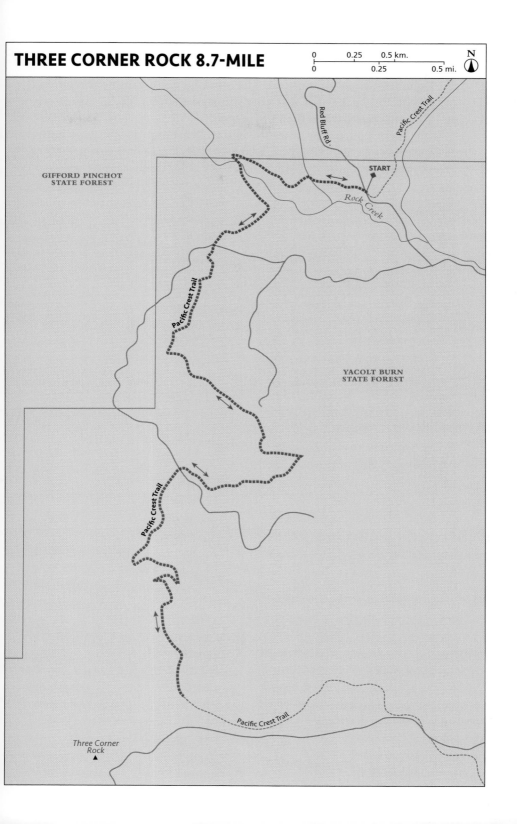

Red Bluff Rd.

Pacific Crest Trail

START

GIFFORD PINCHOT
STATE FOREST

Rock Creek

Pacific Crest Trail

YACOLT BURN
STATE FOREST

Pacific Crest Trail

Pacific Crest Trail

Three Corner
Rock
▲

the Columbia River at your feet. The other bonus of gaining the summit in this out-and-back run is that your return is all downhill, so you merely retrace your steps back to the starting point.

From there you can head to Stevenson, Washington, and get a coffee at Gotta Hava Java (371 WA 14), a beer at Walking Man Brewing (240 1st Street), or a meal at the Crossing (127 SW Russell Avenue).

DOG MOUNTAIN 5.7-MILE

THE RUN DOWN

START: At the Dog Mountain trailhead off WA 14; elevation 154 feet

OVERALL DISTANCE: 5.7 mile keyhole with a loop

APPROXIMATE RUNNING TIME: 100 minutes

DIFFICULTY: Blue

ELEVATION GAIN: 2,762 feet

BEST SEASON TO RUN: Spring and summer for the amazing wildflowers

DOG FRIENDLY: Leashed dogs permitted

PARKING: Free

OTHER USERS: None

CELL PHONE COVERAGE: Poor

MORE INFORMATION: www
.oregonhikers.org/field_guide/
Dog_Mountain_Hike

FINDING THE TRAILHEAD

This popular trailhead is located right off WA 14. Free parking is available right next to the trailhead. Restrooms are also available at the trailhead. If using public transportation, take the Gorge WET Bus.

RUN DESCRIPTION

This singletrack trail begins ascending right from the start. After about 0.5 mile, an option for "more-difficult" or "less-difficult" terrain presents itself via signage. The less-difficult route actually has better views. The trail is forested until you reach the exposed overlooks. As you ascend past tree

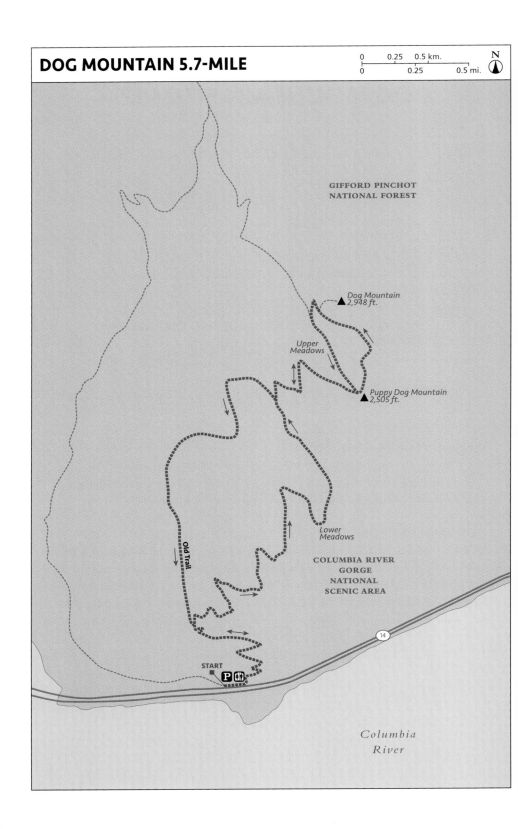

DOG MOUNTAIN 5.7-MILE

0   0.25   0.5 km.
0   0.25   0.5 mi.

N

GIFFORD PINCHOT
NATIONAL FOREST

Dog Mountain
▲ 2,948 ft.

Upper
Meadows

Puppy Dog Mountain
▲ 2,505 ft.

Lower
Meadows

COLUMBIA RIVER
GORGE
NATIONAL
SCENIC AREA

Old Trail

14

START

P

Columbia
River

line, you will be treated to wonderful vistas of the Columbia River Gorge and surrounding mountains. The wildflowers are absolutely amazing in the springtime. Taking the Dog Mountain Trail up and the Augsberger Trail down makes a wonderful loop.

RUNNING GEAR

Eyewear

Running eyewear has progressed enormously in the last decade to the point that sunglasses are now functional and extremely protective (as well as looking pretty cool). Because trail runners constantly use their eyes to scope out their next steps and enjoy the awesome views, the eyes are very valuable assets—and worth preserving. With lighter frames, full protection from harmful ultraviolet rays, and lenses that shield eyes from insects, dirt, and shrubbery, modern glasses are worth wearing. Even on cloudy days or in partially forested areas, a pair of sunglasses is a good addition to your gear. Lighter colored or photochromic lenses that darken when exposed to brighter light may be used, and it is easy to place the glasses atop your head when you don't need the full-on protection of the lenses.

Today's eyewear also tends to be versatile, sporting features such as adjustable bridges and temples and interchangeable lenses to accommodate changes in brightness. Some sports glasses have venting features that prevent lenses from fogging. Other attributes to consider include rubberized bridges to prevent slipping and straight or wraparound frames that relieve temple pressure. Photochromic lenses are particularly well suited for trails because they adjust to the lighting, getting darker when exposed to more sun and lighter (even clear) when in the shade or the dark.

When shopping for trail-running eyewear, look for lenses that offer full UV protection. Sports eyewear prices range dramatically. Make sure the glasses have the features that are most desirable—lightweight, fit, UV protection, and high resolution—before buying a pair of cheap gas station glasses or investing a week's wages in some designer shades.

ELECTRONICS

Although trail runners are better known for their back-to-nature approach and avoiding modern technological devices—especially when compared to road runners, mountain bikers, or triathletes (aka "tri-geeks")—certain gadgets add to the trail-running experience and can be used discreetly or, in some cases, rather boldly, as when shared on social media. A cell phone carried in a hydration pack can be a lifesaver in the event of an emergency, as is the case with a satellite phone or tracker device.

Watches have come a long way since the days of just telling the time of day and perhaps the date. Now they are "wrist-top computers" or "action trackers" capable of telling distance traveled, speed, leg speed cadence, direction, barometric pressure, weather trends, altitude, heart rate, ascent and descent rates; and they can even receive and transmit messages. Whether knowing any of that data is desirable is a subjective question, but some of it can be quite motivational, assist coaches, and make trail runners safer. Trail runners are now able to explore new terrain with fewer worries of getting hopelessly lost or being hit by an unexpected storm. Neither will we have an excuse for being late.

Flashlights and headlamps are important devices for trail runners who run in the dark, especially ultradistance runners who are likely to race or train at night. Many types of flashlights and headlamps are on the market, so weigh anticipated needs against the different attributes of various light sources. A flashlight provides precise directional focus but usually requires one hand to hold it. In contrast, headlamps free the hands, but some runners find the light angle makes it difficult to discern trail obstacles because it shines from above.

Flashlights and headlamps come in different weights, brightnesses, and with a variety of light sources, such as halogen, fluorescent, LED (light-emitting diodes), and conventional and somewhat outdated tungsten bulb lights. These different types of light vary in brightness, energy efficiency, durability, and cost. Some units allow for adjustability in brightness and intensity of focus, while others come with rechargeable battery packs and water-resistant or waterproof qualities.

MISCELLANEOUS GEAR

Thanks to the influence of Nordic skiers, adventure racers, and European trail runners, the use of lightweight trekking poles has increased. Runners use these collapsible poles to help redistribute the workload from their legs to the upper body, especially on ascents. Poles also help with balance. They should be light, sturdy, and easy to carry when not in use. If the poles have baskets, they should be minimal in size to avoid entanglements with brush, trees, and rocks and to reduce awkwardness in use. While sharp points make the poles excellent spears for charging beasts, they can also do a fine job on your own feet.

Trail runners should also consider wearing low-cut gaiters, even when there is no snow around. Gaiters prevent gravel, scree, sand, stones, and dirt from penetrating the ankle collar of shoes, thus relieving trail runners from the frustration of running with a buildup of trail debris at the bottom of their shoes or the annoyance of having to stop to remove the offending substance from shoe and sock. Some trail shoes are now designed with gaiter attachments or snug-fitting ankle collars to prevent any intrusion of debris.

From the safety perspective, trail runners may consider carrying a first aid kit, snakebite kit, or other basic backcountry safety items like a lighter, about 20 feet of lightweight rope, and a Swiss army knife, Leatherman, or other multipurpose tool. Maps are also very useful. It might also be wise to pack a whistle or mace to repel uninvited advances, whether animal or human. Consider bringing duct tape—the universal solution, panacea, and fix-all that works in a pinch as a makeshift gaiter, blister preventer or mender, cut patcher, splint,

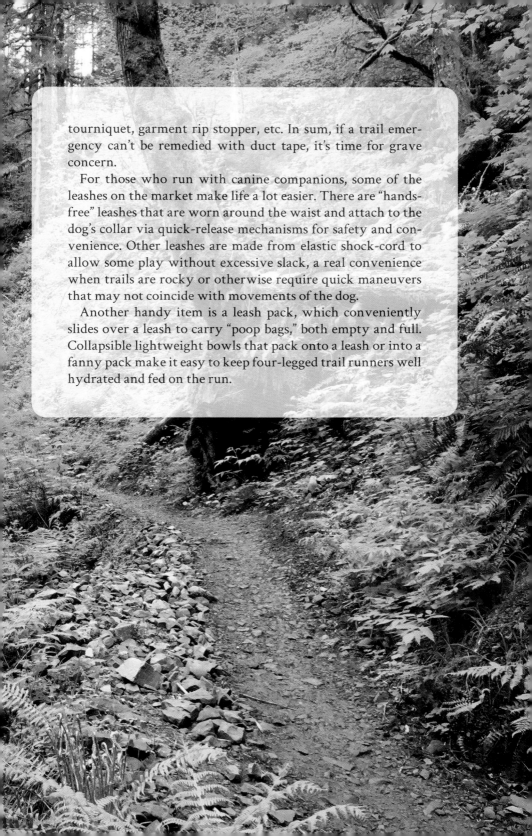

tourniquet, garment rip stopper, etc. In sum, if a trail emergency can't be remedied with duct tape, it's time for grave concern.

For those who run with canine companions, some of the leashes on the market make life a lot easier. There are "hands-free" leashes that are worn around the waist and attach to the dog's collar via quick-release mechanisms for safety and convenience. Other leashes are made from elastic shock-cord to allow some play without excessive slack, a real convenience when trails are rocky or otherwise require quick maneuvers that may not coincide with movements of the dog.

Another handy item is a leash pack, which conveniently slides over a leash to carry "poop bags," both empty and full. Collapsible lightweight bowls that pack onto a leash or into a fanny pack make it easy to keep four-legged trail runners well hydrated and fed on the run.

EAGLE CREEK 10K OUT-AND-BACK

In the Washington State Parks system, Beacon Rock State Park in the Columbia River Gorge encompasses 5,100 acres and offers 8.2 miles of hiking trails and additional biking and equestrian trails.

THE RUN DOWN

START: Eagle Creek Trailhead; elevation 141 feet

OVERALL DISTANCE: 6.2 miles out and back

APPROXIMATE RUNNING TIME: 80 minutes

DIFFICULTY: Blue

ELEVATION GAIN: 1,211 feet

BEST SEASON TO RUN: Year-round

DOG FRIENDLY: Leashed dogs permitted

PARKING: Free

OTHER USERS: None

CELL PHONE COVERAGE: Poor

MORE INFORMATION: http://parks.state.wa.us/474/Beacon-Rock

FINDING THE TRAILHEAD

Take I-84 east from Portland to exit 45/Fish Hatchery. The trail is located near the Columbia River freeway (WA 14), right off the highway. It can be very crowded on the weekends. Eagle Creek Trailhead is the start point.

RUN DESCRIPTION

This is one of the most popular routes in the Columbia River Gorge. This is an out-and-back route, and you can make this run as long or short as you'd like. It is only 2.0 miles out to Punchbowl Falls. This is a quintessential Pacific Northwest trail run, with waterfalls, lush forests, great single-track trails, and rocky footing. If you continue past 7.0 miles you get to run

EAGLE CREEK 10K OUT-AND-BACK

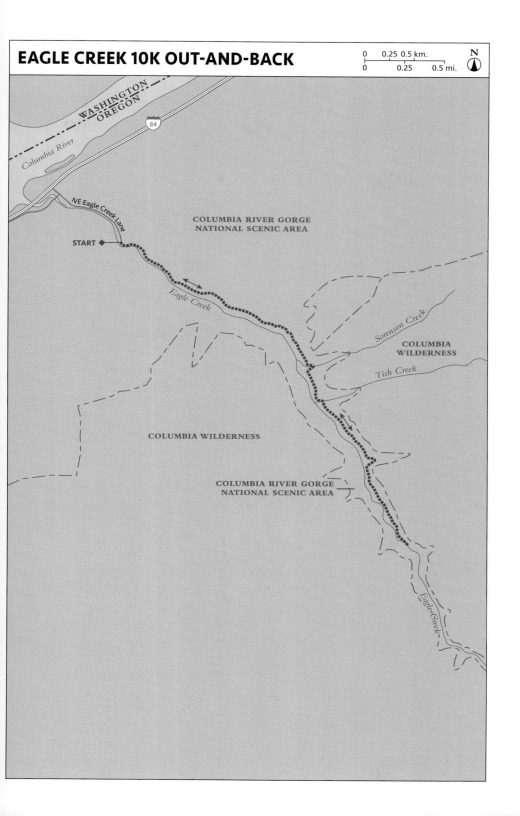

0   0.25 0.5 km.
0   0.25   0.5 mi.

N

WASHINGTON
OREGON
84
Columbia River

NE Eagle Creek Lane

START

COLUMBIA RIVER GORGE
NATIONAL SCENIC AREA

Eagle Creek

Sorenson Creek

COLUMBIA
WILDERNESS

Tish Creek

COLUMBIA WILDERNESS

COLUMBIA RIVER GORGE
NATIONAL SCENIC AREA

Eagle Creek

through Tunnel Falls, an actual tunnel blown out by dynamite that goes behind the waterfall. This area features dangerous dropoffs and technical footing. This trail is also a PCT thru-hiking alternate, since it is so iconic. A lot of thru-hikers take the Eagle Creek Trail down to the town of Cascade Locks.

LOWER LAKE LOOP AT BATTLE GROUND LAKE STATE PARK

Within the 280 acres of Battle Ground Lake State Park are 10 miles of hiking trails, 5 miles of equestrian/bike trails, and a self-guided interpretive trail. There are two primarily singletrack trails around the lake, the Upper Lake Loop and the Lower Lake Loop. There are also multiple access points from the designated camping areas. In addition to the loops around the lake, there are rolling singletrack trails around the park. Much of the trail system is in the forest, so some sections are rooted and can be slick in the winter.

This is a very busy park, primarily with overnight camping, nonmotorized boating, and fishing. However, a dip in the lake after a trail run can be a nice way to reinvigorate your legs.

THE RUN DOWN

START: Off the paved road at the lake; elevation 523 feet

OVERALL DISTANCE: 0.7-mile loop

APPROXIMATE RUNNING TIME: 10 minutes

DIFFICULTY: Green

ELEVATION GAIN: None

BEST SEASON TO RUN: Year-round, but the trail can be muddy in the rainy season

DOG FRIENDLY: Leashed dogs permitted

PARKING: A fee is charged; an annual pass is available

OTHER USERS: Foot traffic only

CELL PHONE COVERAGE: Fair

MORE INFORMATION: http://parks.state.wa.us/472/Battle-Ground-Lake

FINDING THE TRAILHEAD

From Portland, head north on I-5 and take exit 11 toward Battle Ground State Park. Head east and follow the signs approximately 6 miles to the park. The entrance is off NE 249th Street. To access the trail, follow the paved roadway to the lake. Head in a clockwise or

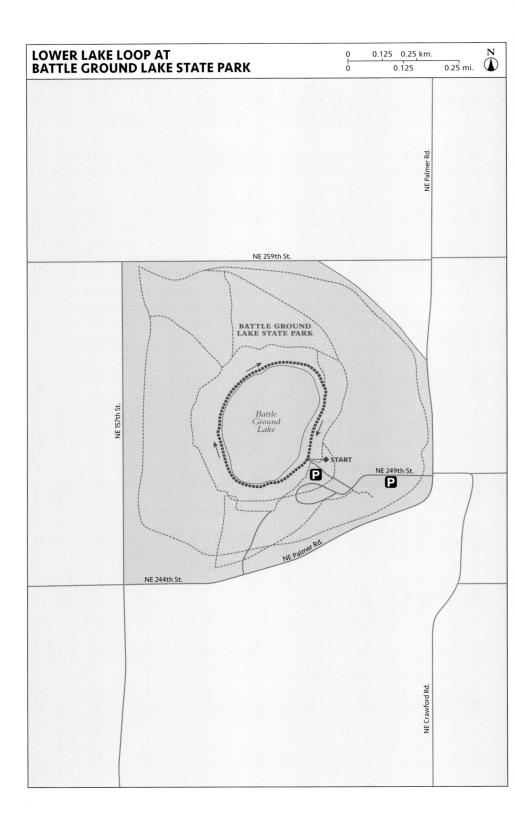

LOWER LAKE LOOP AT
BATTLE GROUND LAKE STATE PARK

0   0.125   0.25 km.

0   0.125   0.25 mi.

N

NE Palmer Rd.

NE 259th St.

BATTLE GROUND
LAKE STATE PARK

NE 157th St.

Battle
Ground
Lake

START

P

NE 249th St.

P

NE Palmer Rd.

NE 244th St.

NE Crawford Rd.

counterclockwise direction on the singletrack trail. There are trail signs on both sides of the roadway.

RUN DESCRIPTION

Running in a clockwise direction, you will encounter some exposed tree roots and rocks that require focus to avoid. There are smooth sections to enable a faster pace. With a bit of climbing and descending, this route can be a good route to practice intervals. The route is well signed and differentiated from the Upper Loop, and the lake is never far from view.

UPPER LAKE LOOP AT BATTLE GROUND LAKE STATE PARK

THE RUN DOWN

START: Off the paved road at the lake; elevation 528 feet

OVERALL DISTANCE: 1.1-mile loop

APPROXIMATE RUNNING TIME: 15 minutes

DIFFICULTY: Green

ELEVATION GAIN: 128 feet

BEST SEASON TO RUN: Year-round, but the trail can be muddy in the rainy season

DOG FRIENDLY: Leashed dogs permitted

PARKING: A fee is charged; an annual pass is available

OTHER USERS: Foot traffic only

CELL PHONE COVERAGE: Fair

MORE INFORMATION: http://parks.state.wa.us/472/Battle-Ground-Lake

FINDING THE TRAILHEAD

From Portland, head north on I-5 and take exit 11 toward Battle Ground State Park. Head east and follow the signs approximately 6 miles to the park. The entrance is off NE 249th Street. To access the trail, follow the paved roadway to the lake. The trail can be accessed in several spots, including a spot near the lake just a short trek up wooden stairs by the roadway.

RUN DESCRIPTION

This route includes some paved sections through the campground and is a mixture of singletrack and wider pathways on rolling terrain.

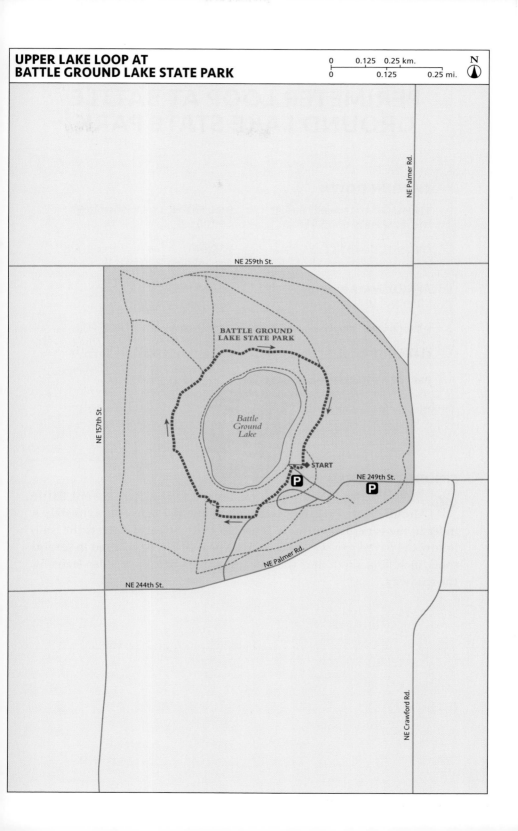

UPPER LAKE LOOP AT
BATTLE GROUND LAKE STATE PARK

0   0.125   0.25 km.

0   0.125   0.25 mi.

N

NE Palmer Rd.

NE 259th St.

BATTLE GROUND
LAKE STATE PARK

NE 157th St.

*Battle
Ground
Lake*

START

P

P

NE 249th St.

NE Palmer Rd.

NE 244th St.

NE Crawford Rd.

PERIMETER LOOP AT BATTLE GROUND LAKE STATE PARK

THE RUN DOWN

START: Off the paved road at the lake; elevation 591 feet

OVERALL DISTANCE: 3.1-mile loop

APPROXIMATE RUNNING TIME: 30 minutes

DIFFICULTY: Green

ELEVATION GAIN: 1,525 feet

BEST SEASON TO RUN: Year-round, but the trail can be muddy in the rainy season

DOG FRIENDLY: Leashed dogs permitted

PARKING: A fee is charged; an annual pass is available

OTHER USERS: Mountain bikers; equestrians

CELL PHONE COVERAGE: Fair

MORE INFORMATION: http://parks.state.wa.us/472/Battle-Ground-Lake

FINDING THE TRAILHEAD

From Portland, head north on I-5 and take exit 11 toward Battle Ground State Park. Head east and follow the signs approximately 6 miles to the park. The entrance is off NE 249th Street. To access the trail, follow the paved roadway to the lake. The trail can be accessed in several spots, including a spot near the lake just a short trek up wooden stairs by the roadway.

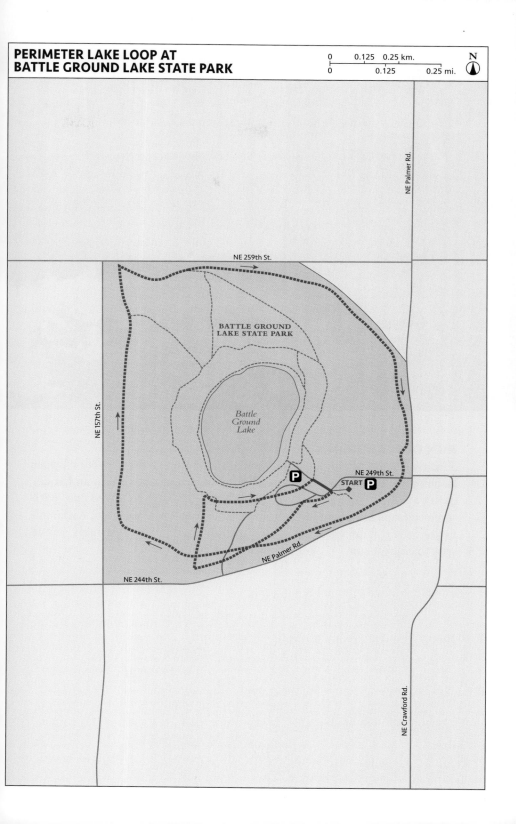

RUN DESCRIPTION

This trail could be run separately or as an addition to the Lower or Upper Loop routes for a longer effort. A mixture of singletrack terrain and wider pathways weaves in and out of the forest. This easily followed run, with some signage, also includes a section through an open meadow. Although never too far from the road leading into the park, it is a relatively serene spot to enjoy a run.

Recovery, Rest, and Common Sense

More is not always better. This is sometimes the most difficult lesson for trail runners to fully absorb. Failure to learn the lesson leads to acute injury or chronic suboptimal performance. Even ultrarunners know that some rest, even if only active rest through cross-training, enhances their running performance. Just as the need exists to integrate recovery and rest into repeat or interval training to get the most from each repeat or interval, periods of recovery and rest should be integrated into your overall training schedule. It often takes more discipline to take a day off than to go hard or long.

With proper recovery and rest, trail runners are able to attack hard days and make them worthwhile. Without recovery and rest, the pace of hard runs and easy runs will be approximately the same, and very little benefit will result from either. If you are the type who is likely to overdo it, keep a running log or journal that tracks your daily runs, noting time, effort, mileage, and other pertinent factors such as weather, cross-training activities, sleep, diet, work load, emotional state, stress level, terrain, and, if you know them, altitude and heart rate. Those daily entries will force you to face the question of whether you are doing quality runs as opposed to sheer quantity. The diary will also give an indication of whether you are overtraining. When you notice progress in your running, you will be in a better position to recall and evaluate what factors worked to produce that success.

Another alternative for those who lack the discipline for proper recovery and rest is to get a coach. Although not many coaches specialize in trail training, a good running coach will be able to help develop a customized training schedule that takes into consideration a runner's personal strengths and weaknesses. A coach should also help integrate recovery days and rest into your training.

Only so much fuel is in any runner's tank, and if it isn't replenished between workouts, that reservoir will soon be running on empty. While it is a worthwhile training experience to overstress your system and run on "fumes," that should be a rare exception rather than the rule. Depriving the body of proper recovery and rest is like running without adequate food or drink; eventually breakdown will occur, at which point you'll have to stop for longer than if you had worked adequate recovery and rest periods into the training schedule.

To assure that easy days or recovery runs are not overly strenuous, arrange to run with someone who is willing to run at a moderate pace. Avoid running with someone who has a proclivity to pick it up or with whom you tend to be competitive. Consider running without a watch, or wear a heart rate monitor that can be set to warn if a predetermined rate is exceeded. Be open to the idea of walking ascents, stopping to stretch, or simply smelling the flowers and enjoying a vista.

A trail runner may boast of having put in a solid month of 120-mile weeks, yet show little to no benefit from such high mileage. Alternatively, a runner who puts in as little as 30 to 40 miles a week in three or four runs can show tremendous progress if each of those runs serves a particular training purpose. Design the easy days to accomplish a purpose, and transfer any pent-up energy to the hard or long days to really make those workouts count toward improvement.

Although trail running may not beat a runner up the way road or track running does, it is still important to incorporate recovery and rest into training. Recovery and rest periods should come between repeats and intervals, between hard workouts, and before and after races. The use of recovery and rest also applies on a macro level, such as in scheduling a particular season or year to build up to a specific running goal. A trail runner often picks a race as far off as a year, then trains with that race in mind, perhaps running several "training" races geared to preparing for "the target" race.

The training principle of "periodization" (also called "phase" training) is based on the idea that an athlete may reach a performance peak by building up through a set of steps, each of which may last for weeks or months, depending on the starting point and where the athlete wants to be at the peak of the periodization training. Periodization training starts with a build-up or foundation period, upon which a base of endurance and strength is built. From there, the athlete works on speed and endurance, incorporating distance, tempo runs, intervals, repeats, and fartleks. Once the fitness and strength levels are sufficient to run the target distance at a pace that is close to the goal, focus is reoriented to speed work and turnover to tweak muscles for a fast pace. It is at this point that the athlete is ready for a recovery phase, also known as the "taper" period.

Within the big picture of a periodization schedule, you should be prepared to make micro adjustments for recovery and rest to stave off overtraining or injury. Know your body and be aware of heightened heart rate, sleep problems, loss of appetite, a short temper, a general lack of enthusiasm, tight or sore muscles, bones, and connective tissue, or other symptoms of burnout. Get adequate sleep with a consistent sleep routine. Quality of rest is probably more important than quantity, and playing catch-up does not always work to restore your body to a rested state. Also be sure to eat a balanced diet with adequate calories and fluids to power through the workout and the entire day.

Engaging in yoga or meditation can play a useful part in the recovery and rest phase. Just because you are not running trails during your time off doesn't mean you must sacrifice the peace of mind gained from running in a beautiful place. Those who practice meditative arts are able to reach a similar state of equanimity and tranquility as that gained by running trails, without lifting a foot. Another restorative measure, if available, is a sauna, hot tub, or steam room. The benefits of sports massage are also likely to be worth the time and cost.

When determining the amount of recovery and rest needed, consider the impact of other life events and the effect that family, work, travel, social, and emotional lives have on training—and vice versa. The need may arise to run more or less during particularly stressful periods, regardless of the specific point in the periodization schedule. If emotionally drained, a long slow run in a scenic environment might replace what was supposed to be a hard hill repeat day.

Know yourself, set reasonable short- and long-term goals, and be willing to adjust them. Be flexible and avoid imposing on yourself a training partner's or someone else's goals. Every trail runner is an individual and responds to different types of training. What works for one trail runner might be a huge mistake for another. Be sensitive to all of your needs, plus those of family, friends, and coworkers.

A holistic approach to trail running will keep training in perspective. Yes, you need to respect the importance of adequate training, but do not miss the forest for the trees. You will be better able to run the trail that leads through those trees if it is done from a more balanced place. In addition to proper form, fitness, strength, nutrition, and gear, athletes become better runners if they are happy with their family and work lives. Avoiding overtraining or chronic fatigue and approaching each run with fervor keep a runner motivated and assure quality training. You will also run more easily if not burdened with stress or lack of recovery, rest, and relaxation. Finally, common sense trumps total exhaustion, lasting pain, and serious injury.

Running trails with a sense of purpose and strength is an invigorating experience that cultivates a deep sensation of satisfaction, one that overflows and leads to a fulfilling life.

RUNS NEAR PORTLAND

HAGG LAKE 15-MILE MUD LOOP

Located about 25 miles from southwest Portland, Hagg Lake Park is a wonderful trail-running destination. The area offers smooth, runnable, and rolling terrain, much of which is singletrack in open meadows as well as forest. There are some short paved sections, including a section over the dam if you run around the entire lake.

The trails afford expansive lake views and deer sightings are common. In addition to circumnavigating the lake, there is a 0.5-mile Interpretive Loop Trail near the Eagle Point Recreation Area that may be accessed from the Lake Trail.

After the run, stop at the Coffee House in the Grove, 1932 21st Avenue in Forest Grove.

THE RUN DOWN

START: Near the Sain Creek Recreation Area pavilion; elevation 351 feet

OVERALL DISTANCE: 15-mile loop

APPROXIMATE RUNNING TIME: 2 hours

DIFFICULTY: Green

ELEVATION GAIN: 1,500 feet

BEST SEASON TO RUN: Year-round

DOG FRIENDLY: Leashed dogs permitted

PARKING: An entrance fee is charged; an annual pass is available

OTHER USERS: Bikers; no equestrian use

CELL PHONE COVERAGE: Poor

MORE INFORMATION: www.co.washington.or.us/hagglake/

HAGG LAKE 15-MILE MUD LOOP

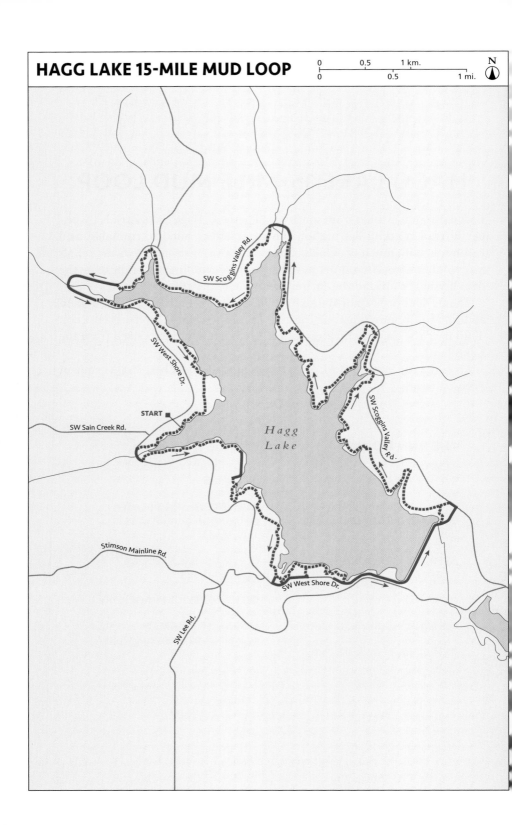

0   0.5   1 km.

0   0.5   1 mi.

SW Scoggins Valley Rd.

SW West Shore Dr.

START

SW Sain Creek Rd.

Hagg
Lake

SW Scoggins Valley Rd.

Stimson Mainline Rd.

SW West Shore Dr.

SW Lee Rd.

FINDING THE TRAILHEAD

Hagg Lake is located approximately 35 miles from downtown Portland. Starting on I-405 headed south from W Burnside Street, go approximately 1 mile to US 26 westbound. From US 26, head south at exit 57, and take NW Zion Church Road, NW Cornelius Schefflin Road, and NW Martin Road to OR 47 S/Quince Street. Turn left onto OR 47 S/Quince Street and continue south. Turn right onto SW Scoggins Valley Road and proceed past the ranger station. Turn left on West Shore Drive, crossing the dam. Continue north for approximately 3.5 miles to the signed Sain Creek Recreation Area, where there is parking. The trailhead is near the pavilion.

RUN DESCRIPTION

This mostly singletrack trail can be muddy in spots during the rainy months. This is a relatively flat loop, with a few slight inclines, making it a green-level beginner run. There is trail signage around the lake to assist with navigation. If running in a clockwise direction, keep the lake to your right.

BEYOND PORTLAND

HAGG LAKE 6-MILE OUT-AND-BACK

THE RUN DOWN

START: Near the Sain Creek Recreation Area pavilion; elevation 354 feet

OVERALL DISTANCE: 6.0 miles out and back

APPROXIMATE RUNNING TIME: 65 minutes

DIFFICULTY: Green

ELEVATION GAIN: 680 feet

BEST SEASON TO RUN: Year-round; can have some very muddy sections in the winter

DOG FRIENDLY: Leashed dogs permitted

PARKING: An entrance fee is charged; an annual pass is available

OTHER USERS: Bikers; no equestrians

CELL PHONE COVERAGE: Poor

MORE INFORMATION: www.co.washington.or.us/hagglake/

FINDING THE TRAILHEAD

Hagg Lake is located approximately 35 miles from downtown Portland. Starting on I-405 headed south from W Burnside Street, go approximately 1 mile to US 26 westbound. From US 26 head south at exit 57, and take NW Zion Church Road, NW Cornelius Schefflin Road, and NW Martin Road to OR 47 S/Quince Street. Turn left onto OR 47 S/Quince Street and continue south. Turn right onto SW Scoggins Valley Road and proceed past the ranger station. Turn left on West Shore Drive, crossing the dam. Continue north for approximately 3.5 miles to the signed Sain Creek Recreation Area, where there is parking. The trailhead is near the pavilion.

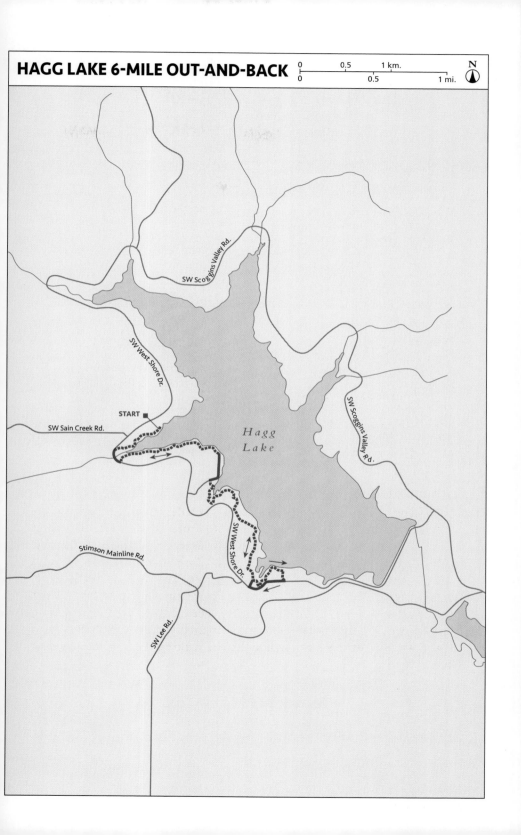

HAGG LAKE 6-MILE OUT-AND-BACK

N

SW Scoggins Valley Rd.

SW West Shore Dr.

START

SW Sain Creek Rd.

SW Scoggins Valley Rd.

Hagg Lake

SW West Shore Dr.

Stimson Mainline Rd.

SW Lee Rd.

RUN DESCRIPTION

The mostly singletrack trail can be muddy in spots during the rainy months. Rolling terrain with some climbing and descending makes this route more challenging than a typical green-level trail run.

HAGG LAKE INTERPRETIVE LOOP TRAIL

THE RUN DOWN

START: In the parking lot just north of the Eagle Point Recreation Area; elevation 399 feet

OVERALL DISTANCE: 0.5-mile loop

APPROXIMATE RUNNING TIME: 10 minutes

DIFFICULTY: Green

ELEVATION GAIN: 78 feet

BEST SEASON TO RUN: Year-round; can have some very muddy sections in the winter

DOG FRIENDLY: Leashed dogs permitted

PARKING: An entrance fee is charged; an annual pass is available

OTHER USERS: Bikers; no equestrians

CELL PHONE COVERAGE: Poor

MORE INFORMATION: www.co .washington.or.us/hagglake/

FINDING THE TRAILHEAD

Hagg Lake is located approximately 35 miles from downtown Portland. Starting on I-405 headed south from W Burnside Street, go approximately 1 mile to US 26 westbound. From US 26 head south at exit 57, and take NW Zion Church Road, NW Cornelius Schefflin Road, and NW Martin Road to OR 47 S/Quince Street. Turn left onto OR 47 S/Quince Street and continue south. Turn right onto SW Scoggins Valley Road and proceed past the ranger station. Park in the lot just north of the Eagle Point Recreation Area. The trailhead is located at the center of the lot on the lakeside.

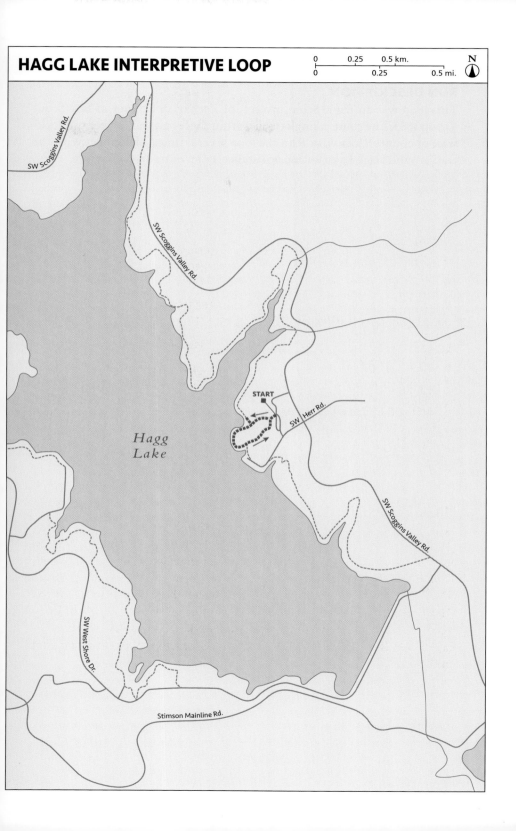

HAGG LAKE INTERPRETIVE LOOP

0   0.25   0.5 km.

0   0.25   0.5 mi.

N

SW Scoggins Valley Rd.

SW Scoggins Valley Rd.

START

SW Herr Rd.

Hagg Lake

SW Scoggins Valley Rd.

SW West Shore Dr.

Stimson Mainline Rd.

RUN DESCRIPTION

This loop was an Eagle Scout project for Zachariah Connor of Boy Scout Troop #855. The route is singletrack within the forest and can be run clockwise or counterclockwise. Run the loop several times, or connect with the trail around Hagg Lake for more distance, or an out-and-back route.

WILSON RIVER 6-MILE OUT-AND-BACK

Tillamook State Forest provides an expansive trail system through canopied forest, complete with footbridges, singletrack terrain, roots, rocks, and healthy, thriving undergrowth. Smooth surfaces mixed with technical terrain require focus, as well as a hearty lung capacity for the steep climbs. There are several trailheads where you can access runs of various levels of difficulty and distance.

THE RUN DOWN

START: At the Tillamook Forest Center; elevation 571 feet

OVERALL DISTANCE: 6.0 miles out and back

APPROXIMATE RUNNING TIME: 80 minutes

DIFFICULTY: Blue

ELEVATION GAIN: 850 feet

BEST SEASON TO RUN: Year-round, but like many trails in the Pacific Northwest, mud and slick spots are common

in the rainy months. At the higher elevations, there can be snow in the winter.

DOG FRIENDLY: Leashed dogs permitted

PARKING: Free

OTHER USERS: Bikes only on Wilson River Trail; no equestrians

CELL PHONE COVERAGE: Poor

MORE INFORMATION: http://tillamookforestcenter.org

FINDING THE TRAILHEAD

Take US 26 west from Portland to OR 6 toward Banks. This trailhead is located about 45 minutes from Portland. Look for the parking lot at the Kings Mountain trailhead, which has restroom facilities. The Tillamook Forest Center is near milepost 22 on OR 6. The trailhead is right at the parking lot. Head up the trail about a quarter-mile to the Wilson River Trail.

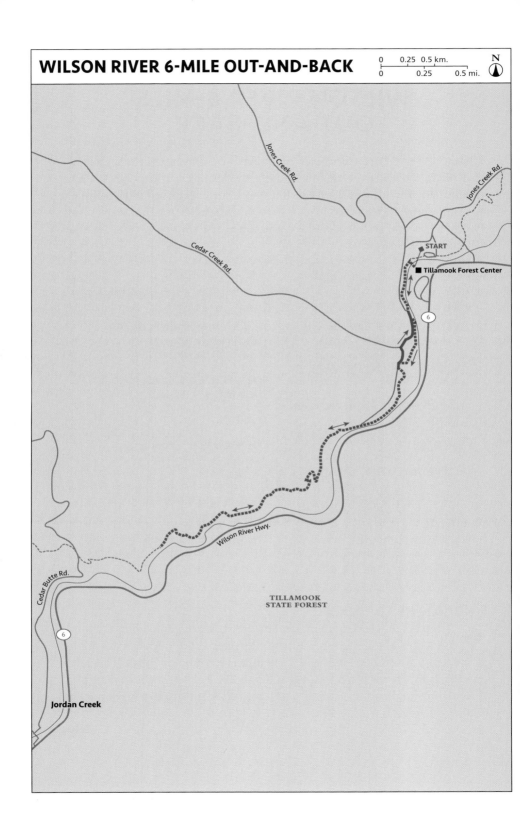

WILSON RIVER 6-MILE OUT-AND-BACK

N

0   0.25 0.5 km.

0   0.25   0.5 mi.

Jones Creek Rd

Jones Creek Rd.

Cedar Creek Rd.

START

■ Tillamook Forest Center

6

Wilson River Hwy.

Cedar Butte Rd.

6

Jordan Creek

TILLAMOOK
STATE FOREST

PORTLAND AREA WEATHER

Many runners "let the weather be their coach," selecting their trail destinations based on whether it is too wet and muddy or cold and icy. Forest runs are especially attractive as a cool respite from occasional hot and humid streaks. Occasional storms can bring strong rain and wind, and the latter may make the forest a dangerous place. Having a tree fall on you can really ruin your day.

Portland runners know to carry adequate rainwear and to dress in layers, because the mistakes of the unprepared may result in uncomfortable—if not severe—lessons. Running with adequate hydration may not be as obvious when there is abundant humidity, but for many of the longer routes we've included in this guide, you should bring fluids, especially if it is likely to take you longer than the projected time or if the day is a hot one.

Because of the likelihood of running across mud, your footwear selection can be crucial. Similarly, if you over- or underdress, that too may ruin your run. Be sure to get your layering dialed in from the outset.

RUN DESCRIPTION

This is an out-and-back run on the Wilson River Trail, a rolling, lush, singletrack trail through dense old-growth forest. There are a few spots where the sun peaks through the trees. Cross the river several times on footbridges as the trail rolls up and down. Although this is a 6-mile out-and-back route as mapped, the length can vary depending on your goals for time and distance. This could be a 20-mile out-and-back run if you choose to run a longer distance.

WILSON RIVER DIAMOND HILL 4.5-MILE

THE RUN DOWN

START: Wilson River trailhead; elevation 571 feet

OVERALL DISTANCE: 4.5-mile loop

APPROXIMATE RUNNING TIME: 75 minutes

DIFFICULTY: Blue

ELEVATION GAIN: 1,330 feet

BEST SEASON TO RUN: Year-round

DOG FRIENDLY: Leashed dogs permitted

PARKING: Free

OTHER USERS: Mountain bikers; no equestrians

CELL PHONE COVERAGE: Poor

MORE INFORMATION: http://tillamookforestcenter.org

FINDING THE TRAILHEAD

Take US 26 west from Portland to OR 6 toward Banks. This trailhead is located about 45 minutes from Portland. Look for the parking lot at the Kings Mountain trailhead, which has restroom facilities. The Tillamook Forest Center is near milepost 22 on OR 6. The trailhead is right at the parking lot. Head up the trail about a quarter-mile to the Wilson River Trail.

RUN DESCRIPTION

Get your climb on with a run up Diamond Hill from the Wilson River trailhead.

From the Tillamook Forest Center, head across the Wilson River bridge and take your first right onto the Wilson Forest Trail. Take two immediate right turns, the second of which is onto James Creek Road, and then make a left at the Wilson River Trail–Kings Mountain Trail, which climbs to rejoin Jones Creek Road for one corner.

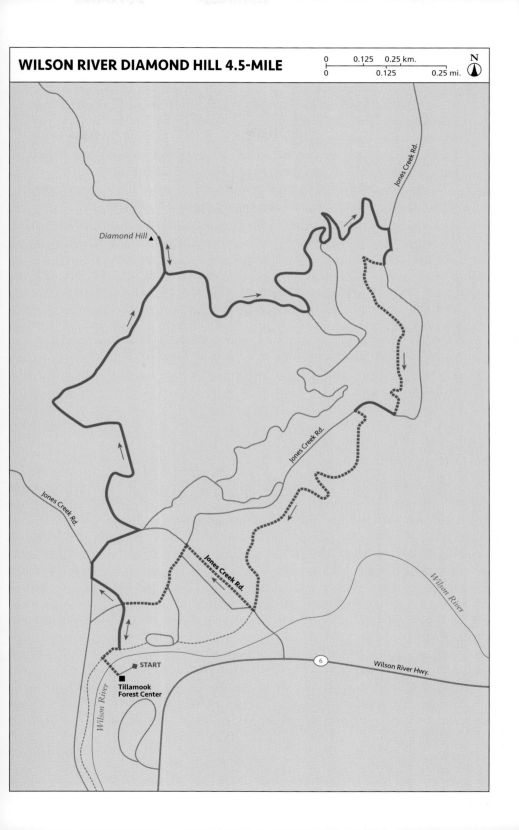

WILSON RIVER DIAMOND HILL 4.5-MILE

0   0.125   0.25 km.
0   0.125   0.25 mi.

N

Jones Creek Rd.

Diamond Hill ▲

Jones Creek Rd

Jones Creek Rd.

Jones Creek Rd.

Wilson River

START

Tillamook
Forest Center

Wilson River

6

Wilson River Hwy.

Look for an immediate left to regain the Wilson River Trail, continuing in the counterclockwise loop by bearing left (to the west) at the first two intersections. The first junction is with Jones Creek Road again, and the second is an immediate left, back onto the Wilson River Trail. Remain on the trail, ascending past two left turns, until you reach a right turn to the top of Diamond Hill. Run a short out-and-back to tag the top.

When you return to the trail, continue in the same counterclockwise direction for your well-earned descent to the start/finish area.

TUALATIN HILLS 4-MILE

Tualatin Hills Nature Center is a 224-acre urban green space featuring nearly 5 miles of trail. Located in the heart of Beaverton, this park offers the perfect destination to enjoy a variety of terrain, from paved pathways to singletrack, all very well signed, complete with several boardwalks amid the lush and canopied forests. Tualatin Hills Nature Park, part of the Tualatin Hills Park & Recreation District, is also the north end of the Westside Trail.

After your run, enjoy a cup of coffee at Bogza Coffee, 12600 Crescent Street #110, in Beaverton.

THE RUN DOWN

START: Trailhead near the main entrance; elevation 220 feet

OVERALL DISTANCE: 4.0-mile loop

APPROXIMATE RUNNING TIME: 50 minutes

DIFFICULTY: Green

ELEVATION GAIN: 397 feet

BEST SEASON TO RUN: Year-round; open from dawn to dusk

DOG FRIENDLY: No dogs allowed

PARKING: Free and ample parking; restroom facilities at trailhead

OTHER USERS: Bikes on paved trails only; no equestrians

CELL PHONE COVERAGE: Fair

MORE INFORMATION: www.thprd.org/parks-and-trails/detail/tualatin-hills-nature-park

FINDING THE TRAILHEAD

Start at the trailhead located near the main entrance at the SW Millikan Way parking lot. The Oak Trail starts at the Merlo Road/SW 158th Avenue MAX Station.

TUALATIN HILLS 4-MILE

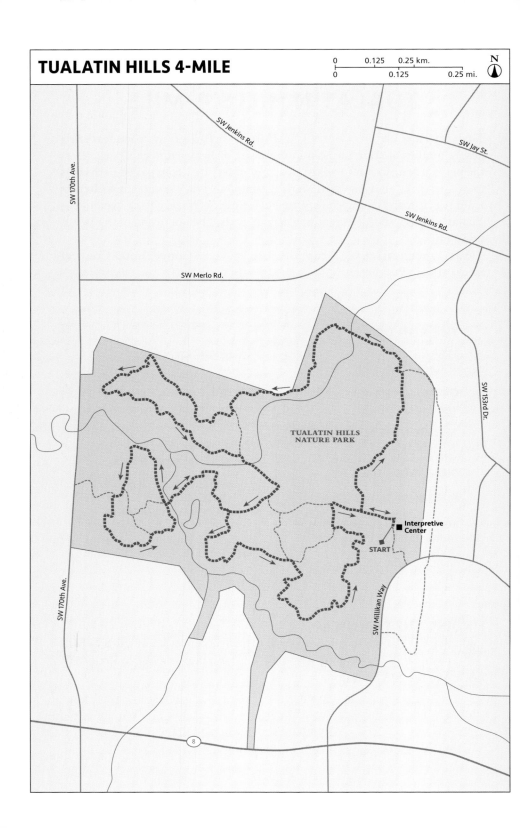

RUN DESCRIPTION

The route is both on dirt and pavement, with wider pathways and single-track trails. The trails are well signed, but carrying a map assists in navigation, as there are several junctions throughout the park. The footbridges can be slippery in wet weather, so take care with your speed when crossing and when turning on and off the bridges. The canopy forest makes this a lush wonderland to enjoy.

From the parking and restroom area, head out on Vine Maple Trail, running due east until you come to a second trail intersection. Take a left on Ponderosa Loop Trail and then another left on a trail with the same name to make the loop longer and continue along the park's perimeter.

The Ponderosa Loop Trail eventually returns to a junction with the inner version of the trail; take a left to get on the left branch of Big Fir Trail, which quickly leads to Trillium Loop Trail, where you take a left turn.

Follow Trillium Loop to Elliot Trail; take a left to Big Fir Trail, which feeds to a short loop, taking lefts on Serviceberry Trail, Ash Trail, and Cougar Trail. Retrace your steps back on Big Fir and Elliot Trails until you come to Vine Maple Trail. Follow Vine Maple to a T with Old Wagon Trail, taking a right turn around to Greek Trail. Greek Trail runs into Oak Trail, where you take a right to head back to Vine Maple Trail—where you complete the big circumnavigation of the park.

WESTSIDE TRAIL END-TO-END

THE RUN DOWN

START: Tualatin Hills parking lot; elevation 187 feet

OVERALL DISTANCE: 6.0 miles one way

APPROXIMATE RUNNING TIME: 65 minutes

DIFFICULTY: Green

ELEVATION GAIN: 630 feet

BEST SEASON TO RUN: Year-round

DOG FRIENDLY: Leashed dogs permitted

PARKING: Free

OTHER USERS: Bikers

CELL PHONE COVERAGE: Excellent

MORE INFORMATION: www .thprd.org/parks-and-trails/ westside-trail

FINDING THE TRAILHEAD

Park at the Tualatin Hills Nature Park to start this run.

RUN DESCRIPTION

The route encompasses Tualatin Hills Nature Park at the north end and Barrows Park at the south end and is mostly on a paved pathway.

After the run, enjoy coffee at the Ava Roasteria, 4655 SW Hall Boulevard in Beaverton.

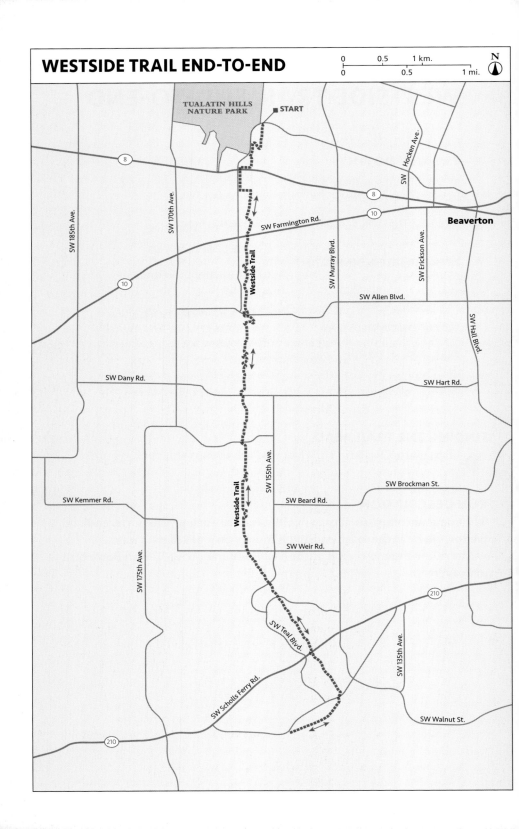

WESTSIDE TRAIL END-TO-END

TUALATIN HILLS
NATURE PARK

■ START

Beaverton

SW Hocken Ave.

SW 185th Ave.

SW 170th Ave.

SW Farmington Rd.

Westside Trail

SW Murray Blvd.

SW Erickson Ave.

SW Hall Blvd.

SW Allen Blvd.

SW Dany Rd.

SW Hart Rd.

SW 155th Ave.

SW Brockman St.

SW Kemmer Rd.

Westside Trail

SW Beard Rd.

SW 175th Ave.

SW Weir Rd.

SW Teal Blvd.

SW 135th Ave.

SW Scholls Ferry Rd.

SW Walnut St.

ROOTS, ROCKS, FALLEN BRANCHES, AND OTHER TRAIL OBSTACLES

When running on a particularly difficult section of trail, it is often beneficial to lift your knees a little higher than usual. This will give your feet more ground clearance to avoid catching a toe or otherwise tripping on a rock, root, or other potential snag. Using the forward vision technique, where your eyes are steps ahead of your feet, anticipating or "setting up" for upcoming obstacles on trail descents, helps select a line in the trail that, in turn, helps to maintain speed without losing balance or twisting an ankle.

Depending on running style, the length of the run, and the distance traveled, trail runners may find it easiest to use a shorter stride and to run through rough footing with lighter but more rapid steps. Running on your forefoot, the way football players—hardly known for their daintiness—run through tire obstacle courses, takes weight off your feet so you can quickly adjust your balance and recover from any misstep. Of course, this is difficult to do when tired and legs and feet feel heavy and sluggish.

Trail runners will probably always wonder whether it is best to jump over, go around, or step on top of a fallen tree, branch, rock, or other obstacle blocking the most direct line of travel along a trail. Even though the decision to jump is driven by numerous factors, trail runners must make the choice instantaneously. Some of the more substantial variables in the

equation are the speed at which you approach the obstacle, the size and stability of the obstacle, your general agility and experience, the footing leading to and from the obstacle, and your general level of chutzpah or cunning.

Once you've made the lightning-fast decision of whether to go over or around an obstacle, embrace it with confidence, then leap over, step on, or steer around the barrier without second-guessing the decision. Don't dwell on a botched decision, but learn from mistakes so you are better able to tackle the next trail barrier. The element of surprise, the challenge of uncertainty, and the never-ending supply of different obstacles are what make trail running exciting. If these uncertainties do not make for fun and excitement, run roads.

COOPER MOUNTAIN 4-MILE (EXPERIENTIAL LOOP)

Located southwest of Beaverton, 231-acre Cooper Mountain Nature Park, with more than 3 miles of trails, is a gem. Opened in 2009 and dedicated as open space, this area offers well-marked, hard-packed, and wide trails that meander in and out of the forest with views of open meadows and the surrounding hillsides. It is a great spot for newcomers to the sport as well as seasoned veterans who want to incorporate speed work into their training on the softer surfaces offered by the trails.

THE RUN DOWN

START: Trailhead near the main entrance; elevation 761 feet

OVERALL DISTANCE: 4.0 miles; keyhole with an additional loop

APPROXIMATE RUNNING TIME: 45 minutes

DIFFICULTY: Green

ELEVATION GAIN: 594 feet

BEST SEASON TO RUN: Year-round

DOG FRIENDLY: No dogs on trails, leashed or otherwise

PARKING: Ample parking; restrooms near trailhead

OTHER USERS: Foot traffic only

CELL PHONE COVERAGE: Good

MORE INFORMATION: www .oregonmetro.gov/parks/ cooper-mountain-nature-park

FINDING THE TRAILHEAD

 Start at the trailhead located near the Cooper Mountain Nature Park main entrance, at the SW Kemmer Road parking lot.

RUN DESCRIPTION

This is an easy-to-follow route with trail markings neatly placed at intersections. The surface varies between packed/crushed gravel and dirt pathways. Rolling terrain makes for an easy-going, pleasant outing.

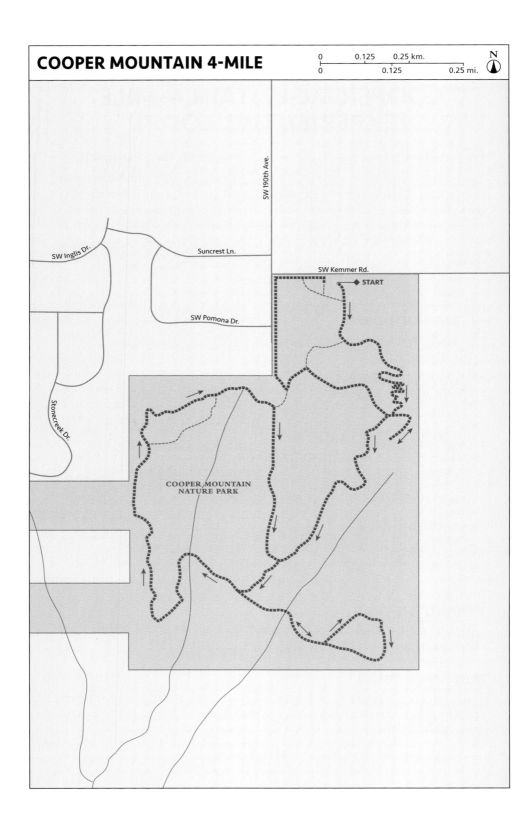

COOPER MOUNTAIN 4-MILE

0   0.125   0.25 km.

0   0.125   0.25 mi.

N

SW 190th Ave.

SW Inglis Dr.

Suncrest Ln.

SW Kemmer Rd.

◆ START

SW Pomona Dr.

Stonecreek Dr.

COOPER MOUNTAIN
NATURE PARK

Begin on the Little Prairie Loop, heading south out of the playground area. Bear left to stay on the clockwise loop, with a tiny dogleg out-and-back at nine o'clock. Jump onto Blacktail Way to continue looping to Cooper Mountain Loop. Run to a T, where you do a short lollipop on Larkspur Loop, and then head back past the juncture to rejoin Cooper Mountain Loop. Stay on Cooper Mountain to eventually reconnect with Blacktail Way, retracing your steps until you run into Little Prairie Loop on your left. Follow Little Prairie until you come to Cooper Mountain Loop as a left turn, and follow the sharp turns until it straightens out along SW 190th Avenue. Make a sharp right at SW Kemmer Road to get back to the starting point.

OXBOW PARK 5.5-MILE

With 1,000 acres, Oxbow Regional Park offers 15 miles of both gentle and steep trails to explore through old-growth redwoods.

THE RUN DOWN

START: 3010 SE Oxbow Pkwy.; elevation 210 feet

OVERALL DISTANCE: 5.5-mile loop

APPROXIMATE RUNNING TIME: 45 to 60 minutes

DIFFICULTY: Green

ELEVATION GAIN: 817 feet

BEST SEASON TO RUN: Year-round, with swimming in warmer months

DOG FRIENDLY: Dogs not allowed

PARKING: A fee per car; an annual pass is available

OTHER USERS: Mountain bikers; no equestrians

MORE INFORMATION: www.oregonmetro.gov/parks/oxbow-regional-park

FINDING THE TRAILHEAD

The park is located 25 miles from Portland at 3010 SE Oxbow Parkway in Gresham.

RUN DESCRIPTION

Enjoy old-growth forest and views overlooking the Sandy River on this windy path that loops through the park. Starting from the terminus of Southeast Oxbow Park Road, keeping the Sandy River to your left, you run a cruiser first mile and then, at mile 1.5, take a sharp left at the T-junction to run up and around the Elk Meadow lollipop loop, which is 2 miles long. That brings you back down to the main trail, which heads toward the river and crisscrosses the road on which you entered before hugging the shore for the final cruiser mile—with the exception of a little climb to return you to the start.

If it is warm enough, enjoy a swim in the cool, snowmelt water accessed from the natural beaches of the Sandy River.

OXBOW PARK 5.5-MILE

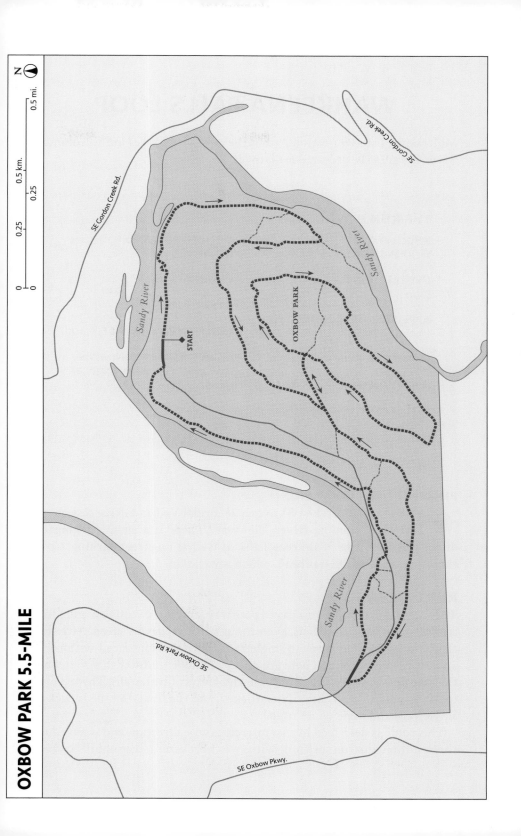

WAHKEENA FALLS LOOP

Multnomah Falls Recreation Area is the most visited area in the Columbia River Gorge, so be prepared for crowds.

THE RUN DOWN

START: Wahkeena Falls trailhead; elevation 106 feet

OVERALL DISTANCE: 4.9-mile loop

APPROXIMATE RUNNING TIME: 1 hour

DIFFICULTY: Blue

ELEVATION GAIN: 2,225 feet

BEST SEASON TO RUN: Springtime

DOG FRIENDLY: Leashed dogs permitted

PARKING: Free

OTHER USERS: None

CELL PHONE COVERAGE: Good

MORE INFORMATION: www .fs.usda.gov/recarea/crgnsa/ recarea/?recid=29998

FINDING THE TRAILHEAD

From Portland, take I-84 to exit 28/Bridal Veil and drive east on the Historic Columbia River Highway. There is a small parking lot directly across from Wahkeena Falls, as well as on-street parking. Cross the street to reach the trailhead, which is well signed.

RUN DESCRIPTION

This route is primarily on a paved pathway, and there is quite a bit of foot traffic to the top of the falls, even though it is relatively steep. After less than 1 mile, the trail turns to singletrack, with portions laced with rocks and exposed tree roots. There are many offshoot trails on this route, but the loop provides a variety of terrain and views of waterfalls. The last mile to Multnomah Falls is heavily trafficked, and the final 0.6 mile is back to singletrack and some wider trail.

This route is described in a counterclockwise direction and is paved for the first three-quarters of a mile with switchbacks on a steep uphill boasting

WAHKEENA FALLS LOOP

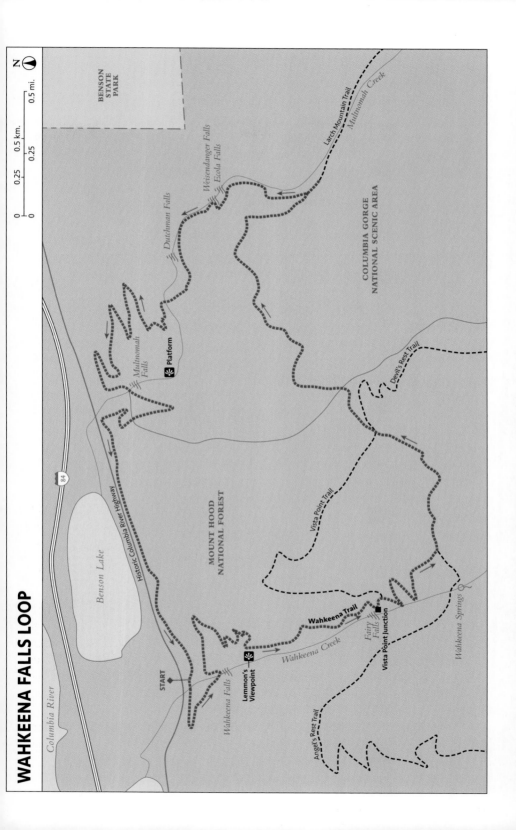

a few spots with a grade of over 30 percent. Once you reach the singletrack, there are some rugged spots on the trail, with exposed tree roots and rocks, as well as views of several waterfalls. The trail reaches pavement for a 1.0-mile stretch to the lodge and visitor center and affords inspiring views of the Multnomah waterfall.

To return to the starting point at Wahkeena Falls, run through the lodge parking lot and continue onto the marked pathway, which is singletrack for a 0.6-mile connection.

MULTNOMAH FALLS TO LARCH MOUNTAIN

THE RUN DOWN

START: Multnomah Falls trailhead; elevation 174 feet

OVERALL DISTANCE: 6 to 7 miles one way or 13 miles out and back

APPROXIMATE RUNNING TIME: 2 hours

DIFFICULTY: Black

ELEVATION GAIN: 4,032 feet

BEST SEASON TO RUN: Year-round, but the upper sections can be snow-packed in winter

DOG FRIENDLY: Leashed dogs permitted

PARKING: Free

OTHER USERS: Bikes on designated trails only; no equestrians

CELL PHONE COVERAGE: Poor

MORE INFORMATION: https://gorgefriends.org/hike-the-gorge/multnomah-falls-to-larch-mountain-via-oneonta-trail.html

FINDING THE TRAILHEAD

From exit 28 off I-84, follow the Historic Columbia River Highway approximately 2.5 miles to the Multnomah Falls trailhead, which is on the south side of the highway. Alternatively, you can park at a pullout on the highway and walk to the trailhead.

RUN DESCRIPTION

Starting at the trailhead, follow the paved trail up the switchbacks all the way to the singletrack Larch Mountain Trail. Gradually climb 4,000 feet to the summit of Larch Mountain and Sherrard Point. Run one way to the summit and get a friend to pick you up on top of Larch Mountain, or gear up for a 13-mile round-trip. Keep in mind that the Larch Mountain Road is closed at signpost 10 from November through May or June, so plan your run accordingly.

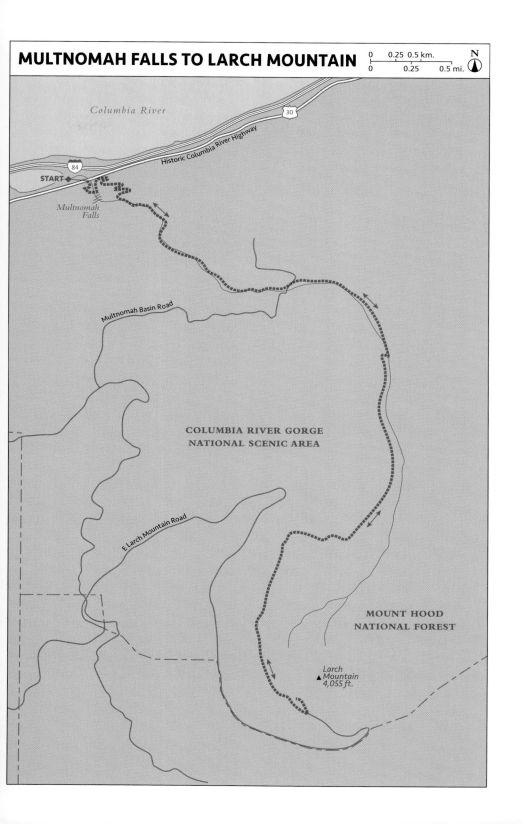

MULTNOMAH FALLS TO LARCH MOUNTAIN

0   0.25 0.5 km.
0   0.25   0.5 mi.

N

Columbia River

30

Historic Columbia River Highway

84

START

Multnomah Falls

Multnomah Basin Road

COLUMBIA RIVER GORGE
NATIONAL SCENIC AREA

E Larch Mountain Road

MOUNT HOOD
NATIONAL FOREST

Larch Mountain
4,055 ft.

The run is mostly on pavement for the first uphill mile, with many switchbacks to lessen the grade, but it is still a steep climb. The pavement turns to singletrack and at times covers rugged terrain for the remainder of the climb to the Larch Mountain summit. Trail signage indicates the junctions along this route. There are some very technical spots on this route, including some talus fields.

MOUNT DEFIANCE SUPER CLIMB 10-MILE

THE RUN DOWN

START: Starvation Creek trailhead; elevation 300 feet

OVERALL DISTANCE: 10.0-mile loop (or out and back)

APPROXIMATE RUNNING TIME: 3 to 4 hours (or more)

DIFFICULTY: Black

ELEVATION GAIN: 4,934 feet

BEST SEASON TO RUN: Any season but winter

DOG FRIENDLY: Leashed dogs permitted

PARKING: Free

OTHER USERS: None

CELL PHONE COVERAGE: Poor

MORE INFORMATION: www
.oregonhikers.org/field_guide/
Mount_Defiance_from_
Columbia_River_Hike

FINDING THE TRAILHEAD

From Portland, take I-84 through the Columbia River Gorge to exit 55. Start at the Starvation Creek trailhead.

RUN DESCRIPTION

This is an out-and-back route, but you can also make it into a loop. If doing the loop, head up the Starvation Creek Trail and down the Mount Defiance Trail (or vice versa). The route offers the steepest continuous climb in the gorge, 4,900 feet of ascent. This translates to about 1,000 feet per mile for steep singletrack that is not too technical, thanks to switchbacks. The majority of the route is within the forest, but you traverse a talus field near the top. At the pinnacle there are some radio towers, which makes for an odd juxtaposition in the middle of open space; but on a clear day the view corridor provides glimpses of Mount Hood and the Columbia River Gorge. Although there is one lake on the Starvation Creek Trail, the majority of the route is void of water, which is rather unique in this region.

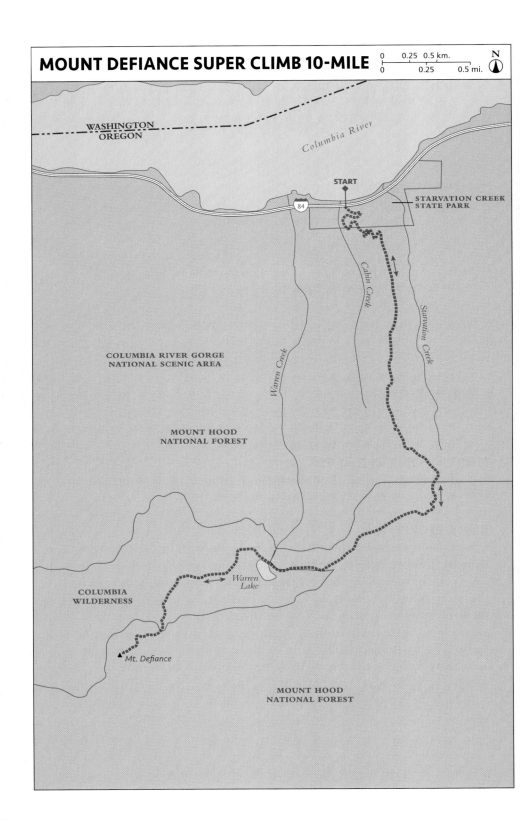

MOUNT DEFIANCE SUPER CLIMB 10-MILE

N

0   0.25 0.5 km.
0   0.25   0.5 mi.

WASHINGTON
OREGON

Columbia River

START

STARVATION CREEK
STATE PARK

84

Cabin Creek

Starvation Creek

Warren Creek

COLUMBIA RIVER GORGE
NATIONAL SCENIC AREA

MOUNT HOOD
NATIONAL FOREST

Warren
Lake

COLUMBIA
WILDERNESS

Mt. Defiance

MOUNT HOOD
NATIONAL FOREST

WHAT TO WEAR ON THE TRAIL

Trail runners often face the difficult "what am I going to wear?" dilemma when they look out the window before a run and try to foresee any temperature changes and anticipate their needs. Layering is a compelling solution to that problem. With different layers of apparel, a trail runner can adjust during the run to moderate temperature, both in response to internal changes in exertion and to external changes in weather. Technologically advanced fabrics have put a new twist to layering, elevating it to a modern art form, the object of which is to find the perfect balance of performance, temperature regulation, moisture control, insulation, and protection from exogenous elements such as wind, snow, and rain.

Layers can be broken into three primary categories: base (against the skin), mid (also known as the insulating, thermal, or performance layer), and outer (shell). While the following discussion is divided into these three categories, keep in mind that several manufacturers, mostly in the outdoor industry, have designed excellent pieces of apparel that blur the layering distinctions by incorporating two or even all three layers into a single garment.

Base Layers and Socks

Worn next to your skin, base layers tend to be soft and are primarily designed to wick moisture from the skin while providing some warmth. Cotton, once very popular among runners as a base layer, is somewhat extinct as a performance fabric and is not recommended as a base layer because it retains moisture, does not breathe well, and becomes abrasive to skin when wet. In contrast, modern merino wool—which does not itch—is an ideal base layer material because it maintains dryness, helps regulate body temperature, and is resistant to bacteria.

The importance of an effective base layer must not be overlooked: A trail runner can wear the most advanced shell on the market, but it will be worthless if the runner is soaking wet on the inside.

Although a fabric's moisture management ability is important, the first priority in a base layer should be the material's ability to help regulate the body's microclimate. Ideally, a base layer maintains a sufficiently warm or cool temperature so that the runner is neither shivering nor sweating. By avoiding overheating, a runner will release less moisture, which helps to maintain better hydration and performance. Nonetheless, since perspiration is a natural component of exertion, an effective base layer regulates the body's microclimate by wicking moisture away from the skin so that it can evaporate or be passed through mid and outer layers.

Base layer fabrics wick moisture through one or a combination of chemical or mechanical techniques. Most technical synthetic base layer fabrics are known as "hydrophobic," which means they repel moisture instead of absorbing it. Polyester, nylon, and polypropylene are the most common hydrophobic fabrics used to draw moisture from the skin and repel it outward, where it evaporates if exposed to the air or transfers to a mid or outer layer where it can be dispersed.

Base layers should be somewhat form-fitting or tight. Some moisture-wicking fabrics work best if they are snug against the skin. That contact allows them to wick moisture at an early stage. Some fabrics are even able to transport moisture while it is in the vapor state. Base layers should fit well with the trail runner's particular body type; and if chafing is a concern, select pieces that use flat seam construction.

When it comes to running in the cold, trail runners can keep their legs warm by choosing between tights and "loose tights" (also called "relaxed fit pants" or "track pants"), all of which are made from wicking base layer fabrics with Lycra, Spandex, or other resilient materials blended in to make them soft, flexible, and quite warm. When it is really cold, double-layer tights, tights with windproof panels, or wind pants over tights usually keep the legs adequately warm. Whether wearing shorts, tights, or pants, consider wearing a base layer of Lycra, Spandex, wind briefs, or wind shorts that feature strategically placed front microfiber panels to protect the more sensitive parts of the anatomy from chilling winds. Wearing fuller cut undershorts as a base layer under tights or running shorts will also reduce inner-thigh chafe. Compression tights, due to their constriction of blood flow, may not have the desired thermal qualities of looser-fitting leggings.

Regardless of aesthetic preferences, the most important qualities in choosing socks for trail running are temperature regulation, moisture management, cushioning, and protection from blisters. Some trail runners prefer thin synthetic socks that have minimal cushioning and offer a better trail "feel." Others find that thicker wool socks maintain a comfortable foot temperature in varying weather, in wet conditions, or on trail runs with water crossings. Those concerned about cushioning may opt for socks that are constructed with various weave patterns in different zones of the footbed to enhance cushioning and comfort. Some trail runners use trail shoes that feature relatively firm midsoles, and temper that rigidity with cushioned socks.

Mid Layer

The second layer, known as the mid, thermal, or performance layer, is a continuation of the base layer in managing moisture. However, the mid layer also provides thermal insulation. Mid layers work with the base layer to transfer moisture to the outer layer and are often made of the same hydrophobic materials, but with a more spacious weave. Fleece, especially microfiber fleece, works well as a mid layer because it has moisture-transfer qualities, boasts a high warmth-to-weight ratio, and is not bulky. Some thermal-layer fabrics use quilted weaves or other patterns that incorporate air pockets for increased warmth.

Outerwear

Finding an ideal outer layer or shell presents the problem of balancing and achieving both breathability and weather resistance. With the goal of keeping you warm and dry by resisting or blocking the elements, such as wind, rain, or snow, the shell must also allow perspiration to escape through vents and technical features of the fabric. Except under extreme conditions, totally waterproof fabrics are overkill and even undesirable for trail runners. Waterproof materials tend to add bulk, inflexibility, expense, and especially reduced breathability to the garment. A stormproof outer layer sounds great for trail runners who confront freezing rain; but if their jackets and pants do not breathe well, those runners quickly become as wet from the inside as they would have had they chosen shells that lacked any water-resistant properties.

In most conditions, trail runners will be served best by microfiber outer layers that allow molecules of body-temperature vapor to escape while being windproof and water resistant rather than waterproof. Microfiber garments are often less expensive, weigh less, pack smaller, and are more pliant and therefore less noisy than their waterproof counterparts. Some manufacturers have applied laminates or encapsulating processes to enhance the windproof qualities and water-resisting performance of microfiber apparel.

Important qualities that distinguish functional trail-running shells from those that are better used for other types of outdoor recreation include the presence and optimum placement of venting systems, pockets, hoods, cuffs, closures, lining, and abrasion-resistant panels. When considering the purchase of a jacket with all the bells and whistles, think about whether the weight and cost of each zippered, snapped, Velcroed, or cord-locked opening is necessary.

Decide what style of shell—pullover "shirts," full-zip jackets, or vests—is best. Also consider the costs and benefits of such features as self-storage pockets and the integration of other fabrics in various panels, such as fleece, stretch material, breathable material, wicking material, or mesh back sections. If night running with motor vehicles is part of the regime, reflective taping is a worthwhile feature. Finally, try on the jacket to check the collar height, and look for the presence of a fleece chin cover to protect you from exposure to or abrasion from cold zipper pulls.

Head and Hands

Trail runners should think twice before setting out on a jaunt without a hat or cap. Caps, especially those with bills, protect the scalp and eyes from sun and reduce the chances of overheating. Many caps are made out of moisture-wicking materials, and some feature mesh sides for venting heat. Some hats are made specifically for blocking the sun, having been constructed of fabric with a high SPF rating, and feature draped flaps that shield the neck from sun rays.

Given that approximately half the body's heat escapes through the head, hats are the single most important item of apparel for maintaining warmth. Many hats can be rolled up or down to expose or cover ears as a means of adjusting for a more comfortable temperature. When running in extreme cold, look for hats that are made with fleece, wind-blocking materials, wool, or a combination of fabrics that preserve warmth yet wick away perspiration under a variety of foul weather conditions. When the temperature is particularly frigid or if the windchill factor makes exposure and frostbite a real danger, it may be necessary to run with a face covering, neck gaiter, or balaclava to protect skin.

Mittens are much warmer than gloves; and if manual dexterity is not a concern, mittens are probably a better choice for colder climes. Some trail runners wear bicycling or weight-lifting gloves with padded palms to protect their hands from falls or when scrambling.

Gloves and mittens are made in a variety of different fabrics and vary in thickness. Some are made of moisture-wicking, windproof, or waterproof fabrics, while others feature high-tech materials that are either integrated into or coat glove or mitten linings to maintain a comfortable temperature. If the hand temperature rises above the engineered comfort zone or "target" temperature, the material absorbs the heat and stores it for subsequent release should the hands cool below the target temperature. As a final consideration, if the backs of mittens or gloves are likely to be used as a nose wipe, make sure the fabric is soft.

MOUNT HOOD
TIMBERLINE LODGE LOOP

THE RUN DOWN

START: Trailhead next to the Timberline Lodge; elevation 5,948 feet

OVERALL DISTANCE: 6.0-mile loop

APPROXIMATE RUNNING TIME: 80 minutes

DIFFICULTY: Blue

ELEVATION GAIN: 1,798 feet

BEST SEASON TO RUN: Summer and fall

DOG FRIENDLY: Leashed dogs permitted

PARKING: Free

OTHER USERS: Mountain bikers on designated trails

CELL PHONE COVERAGE: Good

MORE INFORMATION: www .timberlinelodge.com/ activities/hiking/

FINDING THE TRAILHEAD

Mount Hood Express (public transport) will take runners to the Timberline Lodge from the Sandy, Oregon, bus stop for a low fare. If driving from downtown Portland, take I-84 east toward the Dalles. Turn south on NE Hogan Drive, and continue to US 26 east. Turn left onto the Timberline Highway. The trailhead is right next to the Timberline Lodge.

RUN DESCRIPTION

This loop run is just one of many trail options from the lodge; another popular route is the Paradise Park Loop. A lot of this route is considered high alpine trail running due to the open nature of the area. There is a mixture of singletrack and doubletrack. The trail is fairly smooth, with some loose rock areas, but is not too technical. There are some steeper sections. The

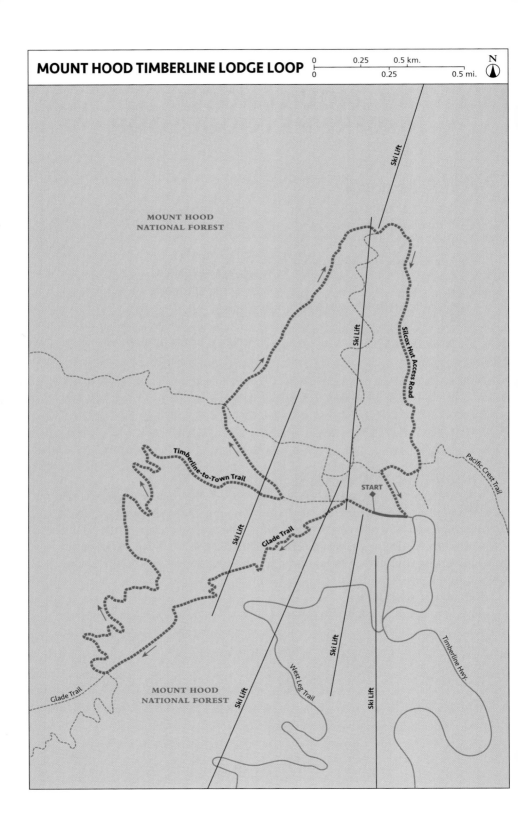

MOUNT HOOD TIMBERLINE LODGE LOOP

0   0.25   0.5 km.
0   0.25   0.5 mi.

N

MOUNT HOOD
NATIONAL FOREST

Ski Lift

Ski Lift

Silcox Hut Access Road

Pacific Crest Trail

START

Timberline-to-Town Trail

Glade Trail

Ski Lift

Glade Trail

MOUNT HOOD
NATIONAL FOREST

Ski Lift

West Leg Trail

Ski Lift

Ski Lift

Timberline Hwy.

trail is at a higher altitude than Portland, and that height offers great views of the Cascade Mountains—Mount Jefferson, Mount Hood, and the Three Sisters. After the run, enjoy a meal at the lodge, and take a special tour of where *The Shining* was filmed.

SILVER FALLS 6-MILE

THE RUN DOWN

START: Silver Falls State Park; elevation 1,447 feet

OVERALL DISTANCE: 6.0-mile loop

APPROXIMATE RUNNING TIME: 90 minutes

DIFFICULTY: Blue

ELEVATION GAIN: 1,024 feet

BEST SEASON TO RUN: Year-round

DOG FRIENDLY: No dogs allowed

PARKING: A fee is charged

OTHER USERS: Bicyclists; equestrians

CELL PHONE COVERAGE: Hit or miss (mostly the latter)

MORE INFORMATION: http://oregonstateparks.org/index.cfm?do=parkPage.dsp_parkPage&parkId=151

FINDING THE TRAILHEAD

Head south on I-5 to the Woodburn exit (#271). Follow signs to OR 214 into Silverton and then to Silver Falls State Park. The day-use area features ample parking, a covered pavilion, and restrooms with showers. This trail is located about an hour from Portland.

RUN DESCRIPTION

The trails that run through this stunning state park, considered one of Oregon's prize jewels, are a combination of gravel, dirt singletracks (some with rocky sections and plenty with mud), and some pavement. From the parking lot, follow the Rim Trail as it heads east, ascending and crossing a couple of park roads in the first mile. Keep following Rim Trail in an easterly direction, with Silver Falls Drive SE to your right. Ignore Canyon Trail on your left, just after a steep descent, unless you want a shortcut that will cut off a mile. Just past the 2.0-mile mark, you'll take a sharp turn to the left on Canyon Trail, continuing down to Silver Creek. Canyon Trail runs next to Silver Creek and eventually loops back to the parking lot to finish in just over 6 miles.

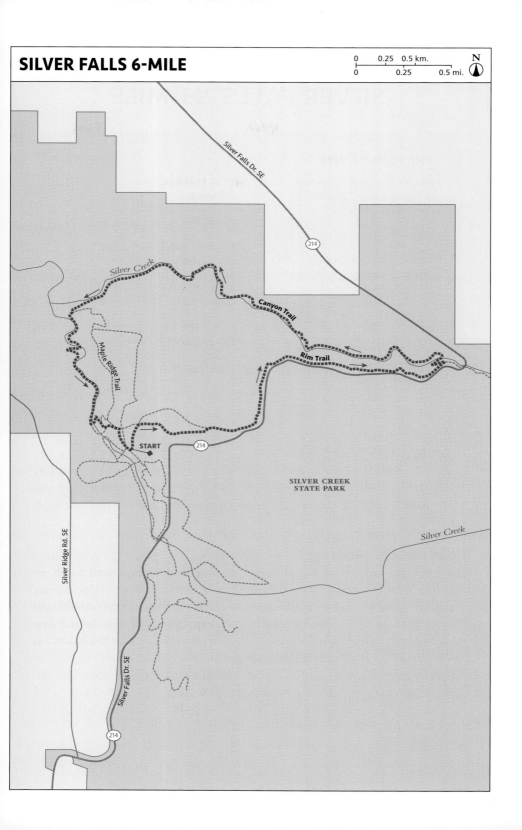

SILVER FALLS 6-MILE

0   0.25   0.5 km.
0   0.25   0.5 mi.

N

Silver Falls Dr. SE

214

Silver Creek

Canyon Trail

Rim Trail

Maple Ridge Trail

START

214

SILVER CREEK
STATE PARK

Silver Creek

Silver Ridge Rd. SE

Silver Falls Dr. SE

214

SILVER FALLS 2.3-MILE

THE RUN DOWN

START: Canyon trailhead in Silver Falls State Park; elevation 1,394 feet

OVERALL DISTANCE: 2.3-mile loop

APPROXIMATE RUNNING TIME: 20 minutes

DIFFICULTY: Green

ELEVATION GAIN: 466 feet

BEST SEASON TO RUN: Year-round

DOG FRIENDLY: No dogs allowed

PARKING: A fee is charged

OTHER USERS: Bicyclists; equestrians

CELL PHONE COVERAGE: Not dependable, some carriers are better than others.

MORE INFORMATION: http://oregonstateparks.org/index.cfm?do=parkPage.dsp_parkPage&parkId=151

FINDING THE TRAILHEAD

Head south on I-5 to the Woodburn exit (#271). Follow signs to OR 214 into Silverton and then to Silver Falls State Park. The day-use area features ample parking, a covered pavilion, and restrooms with showers.

RUN DESCRIPTION

Begin on the northwest side of the smaller parking lot, and head north on Canyon Trail, trending downhill and crossing Silver Creek a little less than a mile into the run. Then, a minute or two farther, take a right onto Maple Ridge Trail, and climb back up as the trail loops you back to your starting point. Almost all of the climbing in this short run occurs in the half-mile after the first mile of gently descending trail.

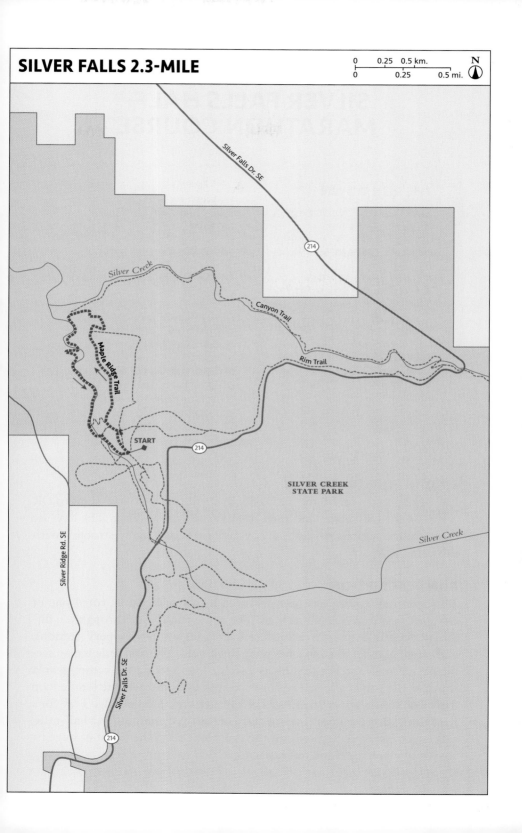

SILVER FALLS 2.3-MILE

SILVER FALLS HALF-MARATHON COURSE

THE RUN DOWN

START: Silver Falls State Park; elevation 1,394 feet

OVERALL DISTANCE: 13.1-mile figure eight

APPROXIMATE RUNNING TIME: 2 hours

DIFFICULTY: Blue

ELEVATION GAIN: 1,804 feet

BEST SEASON TO RUN: Year-round

DOG FRIENDLY: No dogs allowed

PARKING: A fee is charged

OTHER USERS: Bicyclists; equestrians

CELL PHONE COVERAGE: Not dependable, some carriers are better than others.

MORE INFORMATION: http://oregonstateparks.org/index.cfm?do=parkPage.dsp_parkPage&parkId=151

FINDING THE TRAILHEAD

Head south on I-5 to the Woodburn exit (#271). Follow signs to OR 214 into Silverton and then to Silver Falls State Park. The day-use area features ample parking, a covered pavilion, and restrooms with showers.

RUN DESCRIPTION

This stunning course has been featured in magazines and voted one of Oregon's best trail half-marathons. The route runs by or through ten different waterfalls and navigates creek crossings, some slippery sections, and often includes some patches with thick mud. The first mile is on a scenic paved road, and the first 5K is a scenic loop around the camping area south of the parking lots. The route then follows most of the 6-mile loop described above, but at 9.5 miles, take left turn onto Maple Ridge Trail for a hard finish that includes almost a third of the total climbing in a half-mile, spiking at just over 11 miles into the run. Hopefully, the forest of huge fir trees will make the climb feel easier.

SILVER FALLS HALF-MARATHON COURSE

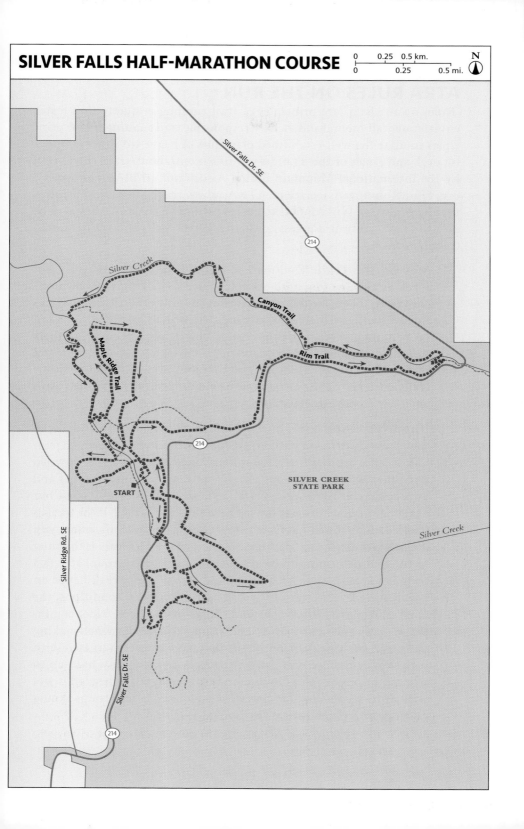

ATRA RULES ON THE RUN

"Rules on the Run" are principles of trail-running etiquette that foster environmentally sound and socially responsible trail running. These principles emulate the well-established principles of Leave No Trace (https://lnt.org), and Rules of the Trail (www.imba.com/about/trail_rules.html) by the International Mountain Biking Association (IMBA). The American Trail Running Association (ATRA; www.trailrunner.com) believes that by educating trail runners to observe Rules on the Run, they will be able to enjoy continued access to their favorite trails and trail-running competitions.

1. **Stay on the Trail:** Well-marked trails already exist; they are not made on the day you head out for a run (i.e., making your own off-trail path). There is nothing cool about running off trail, bushwhacking over and under trees, or cutting switchbacks up the side of a hill or mountain. Such running creates new trails, encourages others to follow in your footsteps (creating unmarked "social trails"), and increases the runner's footprint on the environment. When multiple trails exist, run on the one that is the most worn. Stay off closed trails and obey all posted regulations.

2. **Run over obstacles:** Run single file in the middle of a trail, even when muddy or laden with a fresh blanket of snow. Go through puddles and not around them. Running around mud, rocks, or downed tree limbs widens trails, impacts vegetation, and causes further and unnecessary erosion. Use caution when going over obstacles, but challenge yourself by staying in the middle of the trail. If the terrain is exceedingly muddy, refrain from running on the trails so that you don't create damaging "potholes" in the surface. Moisture is the chief factor that determines how traffic (from any user group) affects a trail. For some soil types, a 100-pound runner can wreak havoc on a trail surface in extremely wet conditions. In dry conditions, the same trail might easily withstand a 1,200-pound horse/rider combination. There are many situational factors to consider when making your trail running decision. Trails that have been constructed with rock work or those with soils that drain quickly may hold up to wet conditions—even a downpour. But, in general, if the trail is wet enough to become muddy and hold puddles, *all* user groups should avoid it until the moisture has drained.

3. **Run Only on Officially Designated Open Trails:** Respect trail and road closures and avoid trespassing on private land. Get permission first to enter and run on private land. Obtain permits or authorizations that may be required for some wilderness areas and managed trail systems. Leave gates as you've found them. If you open a gate, be sure to close it behind you. Make sure the trails you run on are officially designated routes, not user-created routes. When in doubt, ask the land managing agency or individuals responsible for the area you are using.

4. **Respect Animals:** Do not disturb or harass wildlife or livestock. Animals scared by your sudden approach may be dangerous. Give them plenty of room to adjust to you. Avoid trails that cross known wildlife havens during sensitive times such as nesting or mating. When passing horses, use special care and follow directions from the horseback riders. Running cattle is a serious offense. Consider turning around and going another direction when faced with disturbing large herds of animals, especially in winter when animals are highly stressed already.

5. **Keep Your Dog on a Leash:** Unless otherwise posted, keep your dog on a leash and under control at all times. Dogs running off-leash may result in adverse impacts on terrain and wildlife and degrade the outdoor experience of other trail users. If an area is posted "No Dogs," obey signage. This may mean that you leave your dog at home. It is also imperative that you exercise Leave No Trace practices with respect to removing any dog waste, packing out what your dog may leave on the trail. Be prepared with a plastic bag and carry the waste until you come across a proper disposal receptacle.

6. **Don't Startle Other Trail Users:** A quick-moving trail runner, especially one who seemingly emerges from out of nowhere on an unsuspecting trail user, can be quite alarming. Give a courteous and audible announcement well in advance of your presence and intention to pass hikers on the trail, stating something like "On your left" or "Trail" as you approach the trail users. Keep in mind your announcement doesn't work well for those who are wearing headphones and blasting music. When passing, show respect by slowing down or stopping if necessary to prevent accidental contact. Be ready to yield to all other trail users (bikers, hikers, horses) even if you have the posted right of way. Uphill runners yield to downhill runners in most situations.

7. **Be Friendly:** The next step after not startling fellow users is letting them know they have a friend on the trail. Friendly communication is the key when trail users are yielding to one another. A "Thank you" is fitting when others on the trail yield to you. A courteous "Hello, how are you?" shows kindness, which is particularly welcome.

8. **Don't Litter:** Pack out at least as much as you pack in. Gel wrappers with their little torn-off tops and old water bottles don't have a place on the trail. Consider wearing apparel with pockets that zip or a hydration pack that has a place to secure litter you find on the trail. Learn and use minimum-impact techniques to dispose of human waste.

9. **Run in Small Groups:** Split larger groups into smaller groups. Larger groups can be very intimidating to hikers and have a greater environmental impact on trails. Most trail systems, parks, and wilderness areas have limits on group size. Familiarize yourself with the controlling policy and honor it.

10. **Safety:** Know the area you plan to run in and let at least one other person know where you are planning to run and when you expect to return. Run with a buddy if possible. Take a map with you in unfamiliar areas. Be prepared for the weather and conditions prevailing when you start your run, and plan for the worst, given the likely duration of your run. Carry plenty of water, electrolyte replacement drink, or snacks for longer runs. Rescue efforts can be treacherous in remote areas. ATRA does not advise the use of headphones or iPods. The wearer typically hears nothing around them, including approaching wildlife and other humans. The most important safety aspect is to know and respect your limits. Report unusually dangerous, unsafe, or damaging conditions and activities to the proper authorities.

11. **Leave What You Find:** Leave natural or historic objects as you find them. This includes wildflowers and native grasses. Removing or collecting trail markers is serious vandalism that puts others at risk.

12. **Giving Back:** Volunteer, support, and encourage others to participate in trail maintenance days.

Trail Race Etiquette for the Race Direction and Competitor

A few runners simply running on a trail normally have limited negative impacts. All the associated happenings of a trail race "event" add up and contribute to the total impact.

PREPARING FOR THE RACE AND SELECTING A COURSE

1. Involve the community. Make sure you secure all permits, permissions, and insurance. Cooperation from government officials (which may include parks departments, USDA Forest Service, etc.) is a must. Be mindful of potential trail conflicts with other users, which may include hikers, bikers, equestrians, or hunters. Let other public trail and area users know of your event in advance by using the media, postings at trailheads, etc., so that they have a chance to avoid the area during your race and are not surprised by the presence of runners on race day.

2. Select a race course that uses officially designated open public trails. Trail runners may want to test the course before and after the event. Using existing trails has another benefit: The trail bed should be well-established, durable, and firm. If you are using private trails or going through areas that are normally off limits, let runners know this in advance, and strongly discourage them from using the route except on race day. Encourage your race participants to familiarize themselves with the race route only as much as is minimally necessary. Many popular race trails get "loved to death" during training by runners.

3. If existing trails don't offer the mileage or distance you would like to have as part of your course or the type of elevation gains or losses you need, adjust your race distance to accommodate what already exists. ATRA suggests you always use existing trails rather than creating social trails or detours.

4. Think about spectator, crew, and media movement around the course. This can often cause more damage than actual racing. Post signs to direct spectators to other course sections via established paths.

5. Limit the total number of participants allowed in your event in advance. Do not be greedy and blindly accept the number of entrants you might get. Work with land managing agencies to set a number that you, your staff, and the surrounding environment, trails, and

facilities can safely accommodate with limited impact. Strive for quality of runner experience first and quantity of runners later only if increased numbers can be accepted comfortably.

6. Consider encouraging carpooling to your race by allocating preferential parking areas to vehicles with three or more runners, giving cash "gas money" incentives to those runners that carpool, etc.

7. Realize that most people visiting a natural area where your trail race will be held are visiting that area primarily to experience natural sights, sounds, and smells. Most trail race participants value these experiences also. Carefully consider how any "additions" to your event will impact and modify the natural experience for your race participants and others. Do you really need amplified music at the start, finish, and aid stations? Will everyone appreciate cheering spectators? Are banners and mileage markers necessary? Can one course official silently standing at an intersection pointing the way take the place of numerous flagging and ground markings?

8. Consider the timing of your event so as not to conflict with other trail and area users during already heavily used time periods. Scheduling your event in the off-season may avoid potential conflicts.

9. Plan and position your aid stations to minimize conflicts with other users and to avoid environmental impacts. Locate them in areas where access is easy, durable, or previously disturbed surfaces already exist, and away from areas favored by other users (campgrounds, fishing spots, picnic areas, etc.).

10. Plan your start/finish area with care. Is there adequate parking? Will heavy concentrated use damage the vegetation or land? Do restrooms already exist or can they be brought in and removed easily? Is there a wide enough trail (or better yet a road) for the first part of the race to allow the field to spread out and runners to pass before they separate enough to allow safe use of a singletrack trail?

11. If trail or start/finish/aid area conditions cannot accommodate your race without environmental damage (due to mud, high water, downed trees, etc.), consider canceling, rescheduling, or having an alternative route in place for your event.

12. Encourage electronic registration. Post your event entry forms online instead of printing and distributing thousands, or at least print entry forms on recycled paper.

DURING THE RACE

1. Mark the course with ecofriendly markings. These markings may include flour or cake mix (devil's food is great for courses run on snow), colored construction marking tape, paper plates hung on trees with directional arrows, flagging. Remove all markings immediately following the race, but be sure your markers are still in place at race time so runners do not go off course.

2. Provide a large course map at the start/registration area so runners can familiarize themselves with the trail.

3. Don't allow participants to run with their dogs on the course. This is a safety issue for other participants and for the dogs. Dogs also have been known to tow runners to an unfair advantage in a race.

4. Use the race as an opportunity to educate runners and spectators about responsible trail running. Include information about responsible training and volunteerism in each racer's entry packet. If you have a race announcer, provide him or her with a variety of short public messages that talk about responsible use of trails, joining a trail-running club, and volunteering to maintain trails.

5. Encourage local trail advocacy organizations to share their information with the public at your event. If the race includes a product expo, allow local advocacy groups to exhibit without charge.

6. Green the event. Provide adequate portable toilets, drinking water, and trash receptacles. Let runners know where these will be located in advance. Recycle all cans, bottles, paper, and glass. Consider recyclable materials for awards and organic T-shirts for participants. Event organizers and all participants will benefit if they are seen as being at the forefront of energy and materials conservation. As a participant, carry a water bottle and refill at the aid station so you are not using extra cups. As a race director, consider *requiring* participants to start the race with their own fluid and food in a container (water bottle or pack) so as to eliminate the need for cups along the trail. Pack out your gel wrappers and trash. You as the participant should be responsible for your trash.

7. Limit spectator and crew access to points along the course that can safely accommodate them and their vehicles without damage.

Consider prohibiting all spectator and crew access to the trail to preserve the trail experience for the participants and to limit impacts.

8. Promote local recreational trail running by making sure that maps, guidebooks, and brochures are available at the race. Involve local schoolchildren in the event in a kids' run if you have the resources.

9. Stop to help others in need, even while racing, and sacrifice your own event to aid other trail users who might be in trouble.

10. ATRA suggests participants refrain from using iPods/headphones in races. This is foremost a safety issue. Many running insurance providers do not permit use of these devices.

11. When you have two-way traffic, slower runners yield to faster runners, and on ascent/descents, the uphill runner should yield to the downhill runner.

12. Try to be patient when you are part of a conga line on crowded racing trails. Instead of creating social trails by passing a runner above or below the marked trail, yell out, "Trail," and "to your left" or "to your right." If you are the slower runner, stop and step aside to make it easier for the faster runner to overtake you.

13. ATRA does not condone bandit runners (unregistered runners). Not only are bandits a serious safety and liability concern for the race director, often there are limits in races set forth by a permit. Bandits can jeopardize the issuance of future permits.

14. Require runners to follow all race rules, including staying on the designated marked route, packing out everything they started the race with, not having crew/pacers/spectators on the route, etc. Send a strong statement by disqualifying those runners that do not follow the rules.

AFTER THE RACE

1. Do a thorough job of cleaning the start-finish area, parking lots, and repairing and restoring the trails used for the event. Leave the trails in better shape than they were in prior to the race. Document your restoration work with photos.

2. If your event has been financially successful, make a contribution to your local trail-running advocacy group and, if possible, to ATRA,

too. When you do this, send press releases announcing your donations. This will enhance your image in the local community.

3. Get a capable runner to run sweep of your entire race route as soon as possible after the event. This runner can pick up trash, course markings, note any trail damage that needs to be mitigated, gauge reaction from other trail users they encounter, as well as act as a safety net. This runner should carry a pack, cell phone, first aid kit, etc.

ROAD RUNNERS CLUB OF AMERICA (RRCA) GENERAL RUNNING SAFETY TIPS

- **Don't wear headphones.** Use your ears to be aware of your surroundings. Your ears may help you avoid dangers your eyes may miss during evening or early morning runs.

- **Run against traffic so you can observe approaching automobiles.** By facing oncoming traffic, you may be able to react quicker than if it is behind you.

- **Look both ways before crossing.** Be sure the driver of a car acknowledges your right-of-way before crossing in front of a vehicle. Obey traffic signals.

- **Carry identification or write your name, phone number, and blood type on the inside sole of your running shoe.** Include any important medical information.

- **Always stay alert and aware of what's going on around you.** The more aware you are, the less vulnerable you are.

- **Carry a cell phone or change for a phone call.** Know the locations of public phones along your regular route.

- **Trust your intuition about a person or an area.** React on your intuition and avoid a person or situation if you're unsure. If something tells you a situation is not "right," it isn't.

- **Alter or vary your running route pattern**; run in familiar areas if possible. In unfamiliar areas, such as while traveling, contact a local RRCA club or running store. Know where open businesses or stores are located in case of emergency.

- **Run with a partner.** Run with a dog.

- **Write down or leave word of the direction of your run.** Tell friends and family of your favorite running routes.

- **Avoid unpopulated areas, deserted streets, and overgrown trails.** Avoid unlit areas, especially at night. Run clear of parked cars or bushes.

- **Ignore verbal harassment and do not verbally harass others.** Use discretion in acknowledging strangers. Look directly at others and be observant, but keep your distance and keep moving.

- **Wear reflective material if you must run before dawn or after dark.** Avoid running on the street when it is dark.

- Practice memorizing license tags or identifying characteristics of strangers.

- **Carry a noisemaker.** Get training in self-defense.

- **When using multiuse trails, follow the rules of the road.** If you alter your direction, look over your shoulder before crossing the trail to avoid a potential collision with an oncoming cyclist or passing runner.

- **Call police immediately** if something happens to you or someone else, or you notice anyone out of the ordinary. It is important to report incidents immediately.

USEFUL WEBSITES

- www.trailrunner.com
- www.trailrunproject.com
- www.strava.com
- www.trailsandopenspaces.org
- www.rrca.org
- www.bouldercolorado.gov
- www.boulderrunning.com
- www.bouldertrails.org
- http://jeffco.us/open-space/parks/
- www.ci.westminster.co.us/ParksRec/TrailSystem/
- http://highlandsranch.org/services/parks-open-space/trails/
- www.gardenofthegods.com
- www.cospringstrails.com/
- www.cheyennecanon.org
- www.townofpalmerlake.com/
- www.manitoucats.com/
- http://cpw.state.co.us/placestogo/Parks/cheyennemountain